You're the
Daddy

You're the
Daddy

The ultimate guide to being a new dad for blokes

Stephen Giles

WHITE
LADDER
PRESS
new tricks for old dogs

You're the Daddy

This edition first published in Great Britain 2008 by
Crimson Publishing, a division of Crimson Business Ltd
Westminster House
Kew Road
Richmond
Surrey
TW9 2ND

A catalogue record for this book is available from the British library.

ISBN 978 1 905410 41 5

Designed and typeset by Julie Martin Ltd
Cover design by Julie Martin Ltd
Cover photography by Jonathon Bosley
Printed and bound by Mega Printing, Turkey

To our mums –

who had their own battles

Acknowledgements

Thanks as ever to Elle and the boy. I'm indebted to David Burke and Steve Fountain for their wise criticism, to the surveyed fathers for more thought provoking and surprising insights, and to Roni and Rich at White Ladder for everything else.

Contents

Introduction

Maybe you're about to become a father for the first time, maybe your baby is already born, or you're on to the second, third or fourth child. Or maybe you're just hanging around in a bookshop to get out of doing the shopping. Whichever is the case, one thing is true – this book will help you.

This book will help because becoming a dad isn't a simple process – even if you've done it before – nor is it something that comes naturally to most of us. This book will help because there's a whole minefield of new experience out there waiting for you – new stresses, relationship challenges, fears and compromises. As with pregnancy, it's your partner who has the support network and advice on tap. You have instinct, common sense and not a lot else.

But now you have this book – a guide and a fellow traveller to help you negotiate a safe path to happiness.

Most dads-to-be that I've met say they want to be hands-on when the baby arrives. It's a phrase that can mean many things – from dealing with all the nappies and night-time feeds to occasionally bouncing the kid on one knee while watching the football. But generally it suggests a desire to play an important role in the early stages of this new life.

It's an incredible role to play, and each time it is unique and special. But we all come up against the same milestones, the same prejudices and fears. The difference is in the way we handle them – the more prepared we are, the better equipped we'll be to respond in the best way possible. And we're not simply talking about the emotional or practical side of living with a baby, we're also focusing on the other areas of life that are sure to change – from work, your time with your partner and your social life to more concrete issues like how you are going to earn money as a family after the birth, and how you are going to afford the increasingly high price of parenthood.

This book is the honest and sometimes frustrated journal

I kept during my first year as a father – over that time I sampled every style of fatherhood, from the traditional full time working role to acting as main carer for our baby via every possible combination in between. This journal is blended with the multitude of hints, tips and advice I received at the time and after the events. The book also offers the many and varied experiences of other new fathers – my thanks to them once again for agreeing to be interviewed and surveyed and helping to create a really broad picture of new fatherhood.

There is a very deliberate structure to this book, which reflects one of the best pieces of advice I've been given about fatherhood – by a friend who's been there and done it three times over. Fatherhood, said my mate, is all about stages. To start with it can feel like you're only able to think about the next day (or even the next hour), but this soon becomes the next week or the next month as life gradually returns to normal. So the first chapter focuses on the first days, the second on the first night, the third on the first week and so on to one year and beyond. At each stage the art of being a great dad becomes easier, clearer and more rewarding until you have built the most incredible relationship.

In all my conversations and experiences of fatherhood, I've found that one key ingredient for success is confidence. It's hard to get this without experience and it's almost impossible without encouragement, support and enthusiasm. This book tries to offer all three.

So welcome to a new world. It's strange and sometimes unfriendly and it will occasionally leave you feeling lost and hankering for your uncomplicated 'old' life. But I guarantee that, given the chance, you'll find incredible highs and new talents you'd never imagined.

So, life begins. Again.

Chapter One

The first day

"The minute I became a dad I suddenly felt safer and stronger. I was filled with positive thoughts about my family and my future." P, dad of one.

What's Happening?

Day one

Your baby – A newborn baby isn't always the most animated and lively company. For starters the poor little soul is likely to be pretty traumatised by the birth process and may simply want to sleep for the first few hours. Beyond that, the only other demonstrable part of their behaviour is the suck reflex. A newborn will turn instinctively towards a nipple or teat. Immediately after the birth the baby's development is assessed using a series of tests called the Apgar Scale, which checks the normal function of key features like heart rate, breathing, reflexes, skin colour and joint movement. If there's any cause for concern a paediatrician will examine your baby further. Other tests and checks over the first couple of days focus on these key areas, just to check that your baby is developing as expected.

Your partner – She'll probably be exhausted but elated too. She may want to spend most of this first day holding the baby, but this isn't just selfishness on her part. In a practical sense, a breast-feeding mother is the baby's food source, and the two of them need to build a good relationship quickly to help the breastfeeding connection. Your partner may also be suffering from seriously engorged and painful breasts, filled with milk. Regular feeds with the baby will help to ease this.

Last night I became a dad. From what I remember about 11.04pm – the exact time my son was born – there were no trumpets or fireworks, not even much shouting and wailing. I remember thinking it was just after time at the bar. Time to sober up.

I must admit I felt pretty drunk, even though I hadn't been near a pub all day. I'd spent the last hour in an operating theatre, struggling to get my head around the incredible events of the day. It all started when my wife

Elle was made almost immobile due to pelvic pain that affected her throughout pregnancy. She was going through this pain and the agony of contractions for what seemed like ages, before a decision was taken to give her an emergency caesarean section.

In minutes this was done, our son was presented to us and I was sent into a side room while the medical staff stitched up my battered and bruised wife. Then the boy was lowered into my arms for his first man to man cuddle. One sleepy eye peered suspiciously at the bright outside world, the other remained tightly shut, intent on sneaking a bit more kip. Only five minutes old and just like his dad.

Mastering the art

Six goals for a great dad

Let's get straight to the point here – what makes a great dad? The wisdom of all the fathers who have contributed to this book has helped me in my own efforts to improve as a dad and I believe this creates a pretty solid foundation for any new father looking to do his best. There's bound to be things that work for you and things that don't, especially as we all have such unique experiences. But I reckon there are six goals that will provide a good starting point for any and every new dad.

Be there – there's no knowledge without experience, so get stuck in and not just for the good stuff – tackling baths, feeding, nappies and tantrums will bring you closer to your child.

Be consistent – don't undermine your partner, even if this scores you points with the baby. Presenting a united front as parents helps your baby learn and it'll probably save your relationship.

Be cool – give your child the space to develop a distinct personality and try not to project too many of your own hopes and dreams – however much you may yearn for a premiership footballer in the family.

Be flexible – don't stick to a regime for its own sake and don't feel obliged to accept the advice of people who have 'been there, done that'. No-one will think any less of you if you change the way you do things when you hit a brick wall.

Be aware – your role isn't just about relationship building with your child, it's about maintaining existing relationships with your partner, family and friends.

Be confident – fatherhood creates an increased sense of purpose and security. The more you master as a father, the more confident and relaxed you'll become in the role, and the more you will be able to reflect this confidence back to your child's developing personality.

Eventually, Elle and the boy were packed off for the ward
– I stayed with them until they were settled and then I was
asked to leave. I got home around 1am, bleary eyed and
disorientated but still wide awake. Our cold, dark house
was a sudden contrast to the pounding heat and bright
lights of the hospital. I felt dizzy, sick and mentally
exhausted. Which made it the perfect time to ring the
family with the good news.

Hi, it's Stephen. *A very tired 'hello'.* Yeah, just ringing to,
em….*Excited 'yes'.* To tell you….*Impatient 'yes'.* That Elle
has had, that we've, rather, had….*Sound of teeth grinding,
followed by frustrated 'yes'.* A boyby. Baby. A baby boy.

A sigh from me as they paused, then their congratulations
came flooding out, followed by a million little questions
about weight, height, name and voting preference. I
remembered what little I could and pleaded ignorance
of the finer details – including his name, which still
hadn't been decided. I rang my best mate and told him
that I didn't have a clue what I was doing. He seemed to
understand.

After that I drank some liquid, ate some solids, considered
placing all the detergent bottles on a high shelf and round-

ing off the corners on the dining table, decided against, went to stand in the nursery for a while then headed off to bed with *Five-Minute Tales*. I was asleep within four.

The final thing Elle said to me last night was that I should have a lie-in and take my time getting to the hospital. Tempting though this was, I didn't want to sleep through my son's first morning in the world, so I set an alarm. It turned out to be totally unnecessary as the cat woke me at six, scratching at the bedroom door. She needed to go outside, and though she has a perfectly good, and permanently open, window for this purpose, she always likes to make a grand exit through the front door in the mornings.

The dogs, currently holidaying at Hotel Parents-in-law, have equally irritating habits. My life is spent satisfying the strange whims of my hangers-on. Now there's another – and though we've only just met I just know I'll be jumping through hoops to keep him happy for years.

This morning was bright and cold, the kind of weather that would make you feel alive even if you hadn't just been through an incredible life changing experience. I went to the shop to get some drinks and magazines for Elle and just couldn't keep the huge, smug grin off my face. I was desperate for someone I know to show up so I could babble endlessly about our new arrival.

But they didn't, and though it was tempting to bend the ear of the poor woman trapped behind the shop counter, I kept it all in until I got to the hospital. I arrived about three minutes after the start of visiting hours and headed straight for the side ward where they'd wheeled Elle and the boy last night. They'd been the sole inmates then, and I hoped they still were – I wanted today to be about us as a family.

Don't ask the family

Learning the ropes in privacy

The one part of becoming a dad I get pretty obsessed with is the few hours or couple of days spent together in the hospital or at home after the birth – it is such a crucial time for bonding, and you should resist the urge to let anyone spoil it.

The family-free hospital. It's so important to put your new family first. Friends, relations and well-wishers are wonderful people to have around and they add much to the experience, but unless they are blessed with the patience and tact of saints they will muscle in on bonding time that should be yours and yours alone. The only way we could guarantee this was to ban all family and friends from the hospital – and it's something I totally recommend. It doesn't mean you have to exclude the family altogether, as they can play an important (and absorbing) part looking after pets, houses or other children while you're focused on the new arrival.

It also depends on individual circumstances – if your partner is to stay in hospital for a week that's a long time to keep new grandparents away, if she's out within hours then you might want to allow family to visit during your brief time in hospital, then insist on a couple of days' privacy when she gets home. But whether you're at home or on the ward, I'd urge you to 'ring-fence' some time to learn all the tricks of the trade in total isolation.

Home life. The first few hours at home won't shape your parenting for ever, but they might set the pattern for the next couple of weeks. You've got a balancing act on your hands – now is a good time to get good at key baby care techniques, but you've also got to be aware that you're not stepping between mother and child. Elle said later that she wanted to keep the baby to herself as much as possible over the first couple of days, which is totally understandable, though not necessarily logical.

Try to be a part of everything in the first few hours at home because, however you plan to divide the childcare in the future, this time is about bonding, and both parents need an equal chance. Your partner is likely to be emotional, so tact is needed here, but she'll also be pretty exhausted, which is where you can help out and take your chance for quality time with the baby. So dive in at the deep end – the longer you wait to get involved, the harder it will be.

Double your pressure, double your fun. This is a good point to include all those blokes who have just about managed to pick themselves up off the floor after the news, some six months previously, that they are having twins. Once the new arrivals have made an appearance (usually earlier than most at around 36-37 weeks) there will be a great deal of managing of resources to ensure the babies get decent, balanced care. It isn't simply the case that twins are twice the effort, in some aspects they are incredibly challenging – for example trying to bottle feed two babies at the same time is a feat of acrobatic skill – but in others their double act makes life easier. This is certainly true later in their development when they may need to spend a fair bit of time playing together while you get a rest. Twins seem to get less bored than single babies. In these early days, life for you and your partner will be harder as you try to get two babies into the same regularised eating and sleeping regime. You'll need to try and take on one baby each, but also keep swapping the care around so that you both get bonding time with each child. Don't be tempted to economise by only getting one set of baby kit and taking it in turns to use it, the simple truth is that the more you can get your twins in tune, the easier your life will become. And finally, get help, get lots and lots of help from whoever you can. Seek out twins and multiple births support groups – the antenatal clinic in the hospital usually has loads of details on file.

I marched confidently down the corridor, full of pride and nervous anticipation. I peered into side wards where pasty-faced new mothers sat up in beds, hemmed in by semicircles of family and friends passing round babies like fire buckets. The beds were surrounded by balloons, bedside tables groaned under the weight of cellophane wrapped bouquets of flowers. Eternity rings and lockets glinted in the light. Teddy bears stared blankly at me as I passed. I looked down at my carrier bag – three bottles of water for the price of two, a Radio Times to replace the out of date copy I sent Elle in with, a newspaper (for me) and two bars of chocolate, both of which I'd hoped to eat while she was busy. It was just possible I'd made my first big mistake as a father.

When I got to the ward, they were still alone. This was great, as it meant we had private family time and eased the chance of balloon envy. Anyway, Elle has all the gifts she wants – our boy and a gradual easing of the nasty joint pain that's kept her on crutches for weeks. This morning she was relaxed, tired and very happy. The boy was sleeping peacefully in a plastic fish tank next to the bed. I was the only one who was a bundle of nerves.

We sat and whispered for a while. The most important topic was his name. We still hadn't decided, though we'd ruled out many using the tried and tested method of 'did you hate someone at school with that name'? My list ran into hundreds, with the notable exception of Oliver. Elle agreed. After weeks of negotiation and research, it was as simple as that.

Oliver slept on, unaware that we'd finally reached such a crucial decision. Elle admitted that she'd had a sleepless night, due in part to Oliver's occasional waking periods, but also to the sheer excitement and wonder of having him alongside her. I said she should have a nap, that I'd watch Oliver if he woke. She smiled, turned her back to me and was snoring gently in an instant. Bugger. What if he did wake? What was I going to do then?

The cogs in my brain must be louder than I realise,

because within a few minutes he was shifting about. He didn't cry, it was more of a vague moan, but it was enough to make his mother sit bolt upright in bed, shaken from her sleep. I'd hardly even left the chair and she was halfway to his tank. She stopped, paused and looked at me sheepishly.

"Go on," she said. "You go."

So I picked him up. Though it wasn't the first time I'd held him, I was almost shaking with nerves. I wanted to get it right, to show Elle that I knew what I was doing. I put one hand under his head and one under his bottom, then realised I was holding him at arms' length and could do nothing about it except put him back down or stay like that forever. I looked up, lost, and Elle scooped him gently from my useless grasp, backed me into the chair, showed me how to crook my arm to make a rest for his head and shoulders and then she laid him down on my lap. Sitting was a lot better than standing – I felt much more in control. Oliver peered at me with the same suspicion that he'd shown last night and then went back to sleep.

I've always laughed at the dumb statements new parents

come out with, especially the arrogant belief that their kids have perfect fingers, toes, mouths, noses etc. These comments seem even more stupid now, given that no other child could possibly match the perfection of Oliver's fingers, toes, mouth, nose, ears, legs, arms, body and head. And did I mention his beautiful eyes? Even his hair, dark and matted with unidentified gunk last night, is now cleaned to the kind of straw blond that has a true great-ness about it. I sat and wondered at this supreme being as he huffed and puffed and wriggled, no doubt wondering why he wasn't lying in his cosy fish tank.

Within a few minutes he was back in the tank, in a deep sleep. Elle was snoozing again and I was reading the news-paper as quietly as possible. Family life had begun.

A midwife came into the room and rustled up to the bed – they must give them standard issue paper knickers. She leaned across Elle and said "Is she sleeping?" in the kind of gentle stage whisper that would have reached Row Z of Wembley Stadium.

"Not any more, you clumsy, foghorn voiced idiot," I would have said, given half the chance. But Elle cut me off, springing up again like a jack-in-the-box.

"Thought you'd like a shower," the midwife said.

"Not as much as she'd like some sleep," I replied, triumphantly. So what if they'd already left the room by then, I'd made my point. Elle, walking without her crutches for the first time in weeks, looked back at me from the doorway and smiled. I smiled back and nodded confidently. It was a nod that said 'take your time, have fun – and relax, all will be well'. How can one nod get so many things so wrong?

Two or three minutes passed, just long enough for Elle to get out of screaming range, then the first tremor hit. It was almost nothing – if the ward had been busy it might have gone unheard, but in the silence it rang out like a gunshot. Oliver shifted and started to moan. I poked my head into the tank. It hadn't sounded good and it didn't smell too great either. Using the latest keyhole surgery techniques I undid the miniature poppers on his sleep suit, then repeated the process on his body suit. It was like pass the parcel played in hell – the closer I got to the prize, the more I wanted the music to stop so I could offload the problem. But no-one was in sight.

I'd reached the nappy. I decided that an uncomfortable,

full nappy would be a horrible thing to stay in for any length of time, so I whipped it straight off. To my surprise it contained a black, sticky tar-like mess that was now all over Oliver, his clothes and his bed sheet. His judging eyes stared straight at me. I could tell he was contemplating his first word.

I ran across the ward with the little tin tray that the midwife gave us for nappy changes, filled it at the tap and ran back. In the meantime, enjoying the sudden freedom of airing his private parts, he'd peed all over himself too. I took off his sodden clothes and laid him back down on a clean corner of the tank. I had to fill another tin tray with washing water. Back I went.

By this point Oliver was, quite understandably, upset. I wasn't exactly whistling happily either. Keeping up a faint soundtrack of 'shit, shit, shit, shit, shit', I dabbed pathetically at his business end, cleaned him up and somehow dressed him in a new nappy. After a desperate hunt through his bag, I found some fresh clothes and wrestled them onto him. By the time I'd picked him up, cuddled him and stopped his crying our corner of the ward looked a bit like a landfill site that had been struck by a typhoon.

I stuck a towel in his cot, put him back in, tidied up and then, as if on cue, Elle wandered slowly back onto the ward.

"Alright?" she said. I just nodded.

A little while later a midwife came to show us how to bath Oliver and change his nappy. I'm sure she wondered why I kept giving little bitter laughs at her advice. But I also made sure I was listening very carefully.

Oh. My. God.

An introduction to baby care.

It doesn't matter what the classes and books tell you, there's no substitute for experience when it comes to baby care. It's impossible to recreate the art of putting a nappy on a screaming child without using an actual screaming child, so your best bet is to wait until you're presented with a real baby before you try.

However, that doesn't mean you're on your own – the midwives and auxiliary nurses on the maternity wing are there to offer basic advice on baby care and it doesn't reflect badly on you if you feel you need it, because we all do. Depending on how difficult your partner's labour was and how long you can cope with relatives in your house, there will almost certainly be a time in the next few days when you have to roll up your sleeves and change a nappy, or wash and dress the baby. So here's how to get it right:

Nappies. There are two key things to remember – be prepared and don't panic. Before you start on the nappy, ensure you have all the necessary tools to hand – nappy, nappy bags, wipes or cotton wool and water, towel, clothes etc. You can't leave a baby, even a newborn, lying on a changing table while you go off hunting for kit. Be calm, relaxed and businesslike. It's a matter of trust, if you can make the baby believe you are in control, then all will be well.

Once you've assembled all your kit, take off the dirty nappy and clean up the mess around your baby's bottom and genitals thoroughly using cotton wool and water or wipes. For girls wipe away from the vagina to prevent infection, for boys clean around the foreskin but don't pull it back. If it's just a wee nappy and not a poo nappy, you still need to wipe the skin carefully to prevent nappy rash. Let the skin dry in the fresh air for a bit before putting the new nappy on.

The type of nappy you choose is obviously down to your personal and environmental views. Disposable nappies, though arguably bad for the environment, have one fantastic feature – they usually have a cartoon of happy woodland creatures on the front. This gives the clueless father – i.e. me – a chance to get the nappy the right way round without patronising him with the words 'front' and 'back' stamped somewhere prominent. They have a pretty logical structure with two bits of tape which attach to the front panel to form a secure bond. Reusable nappies work on a similar principle but use a nappy pin to connect the sides of the nappy to the front. Don't make the nappy too tight and be careful about the baby's belly button. The umbilical cord stump will still be in place – it'll be going black and falling off over the next couple of weeks – and may be sore if poked and prodded.

Put the dirty disposable nappy in the bin, wrapped and tied in a plastic bag. If you have a reusable nappy, tip the solid contents down the loo and rinse off the nappy. Then wash the nappy using non-biological washing powder. Alternatively, if you want to be eco-friendly but don't want to be up to your elbows in shit, use a reusable nappy delivery and collection service.

Bathing. The same basic principle is at work here – be prepared and in control. Washing should be a daily activity, but bathing shouldn't. To wash your baby's face and neck, which can get a bit dirty from feeding, use cotton wool dipped in water and gently wipe over the skin. Use a different bit of cotton wool and different water to wipe the business end of the baby – a 'top and tail' bowl can be useful, or just two colour-coded bowls.

Baby baths are a bit of a waste of money and are a hassle to fill and empty, so bathe your baby in a large sink or in the regular bath. Support the baby's head and neck at all times, using your free hand to wash the baby. When you're at home it's actually far easier to just get into the bath with the baby and this might help to ease any fear of water. Don't use soap on the baby's face and use only gentle baby shampoo on hair.

Make sure you've got a soft and warm baby towel easily to hand as your baby can get really cold, really quickly. Likewise, make sure you've got some dry, clean clothes ready to go when you get out of the bath.

After a morning of non-stop excitement, this afternoon has been a gentle process of getting used to each other. We took a long family stroll all the way to the TV room and we rang Elle's parents. We went back to the TV room and watched the rugby for a while. In spite of my excitement at being a proud dad my tiredness was starting to show. The emotions that kept me going throughout yesterday's long session have virtually shut me down today. By teatime all I could think of was a comfy sofa, football on the TV and hour-long phone calls to family and friends to boast about Oliver.

Elle said she didn't mind me going – I think she's looking forward to a few hours with him on her own again. She's been brilliant today – hands-off, patient, tolerant – all the things I've needed to get confident handling Oliver. While a small part of me feels guilty for not allowing friends and family into the hospital, I also know if we'd allowed them to take over this practice session, I wouldn't have stood a chance.

However great it's been, time in the hospital doesn't compare one bit to time at home, and I can't wait for them to be set free. The midwife thought it might be possible for them to come home tomorrow, which would be great, but I'm worried about Elle leaving hospital before she's ready, then ending up flat on her back in bed for a month.

The original plan was for her to move to a cottage hospital run by midwives, where she could rest and bond with Oliver. But a few days of cranked up heat, crazy inmates and inedible food has changed our thinking dramatically.

Care in the community

Your partner's options in hospital

Convalescent hospitals run by midwives are a great stepping stone if your partner's had a tough time during labour – and they offer a lot more baby care support. It's a more intimate and focused setting than a general hospital. On the downside they can leave you feeling pretty detached from the first few days of parenthood, and they may insist that friends and relatives stay away for the whole time.

In all honesty it's got to be your partner's choice – you may want her home out of a genuine desire to care for her and the baby, or just because you've run out of food and can't operate the tin opener. Bearing in mind the strain she's just been under, don't deny her the chance to take it easy if she wants to – there will be precious little time for rest at home.

If your partner's had a caesarean section there are some other factors to bear in mind – she won't be able to lift heavy objects and may even struggle to lift or carry the baby. She won't be able to drive for six weeks. Under these circumstances, it's only really fair to bring her home if you're willing and able to take on the lion's share of work for the first month or more – and that's not likely to be practical. A preferable option after caesarean might be to entrust your partner's care to the convalescent hospital for the first week, then take your two weeks' paternity leave. That gives her three weeks to get more mobile and eases the stress on you.

The midwives weren't certain Elle would be signed off today, but we made our intent clear – all packed and ready to go by about 11am. That's made the day long and frustrating, because we've had to wait for the doctor in charge to come and have a poke at Oliver to check that he's doing OK, and then another wait for Elle to be signed off. Yet again, they didn't get much sleep last night, mainly because their was a loud, drunken woman running around the ward – and I thought consultants only worked regular hours – so Elle's especially tired and fed up with the hospital.

But shortly after watching Elle do battle with another inedible lunch I was given the nod and got the chance to settle Oliver into his car seat, ready for the off. He looked so small and vulnerable in it that I immediately began to question the idea of allowing him in or near a car driven by me. Far safer for Oliver and Elle to walk the five miles or so home. Sadly, she didn't see things the same way, so we went for the car option.

The first day

We said quick goodbyes to the midwives and hurried off, feeling like con-artists who've just stolen a priceless masterpiece. I got to carry Oliver in his seat, facing out so that the general public could catch their first glimpse of the prodigal son. Amazingly, there were no crowds of adoring well-wishers pushing against crash barriers and no photographers on step ladders. In fact there was no-one at all – which only increased the feeling that we were stealing this fragile baby from under the noses of the authorities.

Once we were all safely in the car, I made my slow getaway. All I needed was the canvas flat cap and the tartan rug on my parcel shelf and I'd have been the ultimate Sunday driver. I mirrored, signalled and manoeuvred with a care that hasn't been seen since my driving test. I finally found fourth gear on the dual carriageway, while waving politely to the elderly cyclist shaking his fist at me as he overtook. My driving may have been cautious, but I was overwhelmed by the sense of self-righteousness that goes with care of a precious cargo. I finally understand the reason behind 'baby on board' stickers. That still doesn't mean I want one.

As we pulled up outside the house I saw a familiar car

parked next door. It was our former neighbours, who moved out a couple of weeks ago. New parents themselves, with a six week old baby, they'd popped over to pick up their mail. As we were unpacking the car, they came round to see us and coo over Oliver.

"He's gorgeous," they said. And I'm fairly sure I picked up a sizeable degree of envy.

"Yes," I felt like saying, "but I'm sure your child will still have some sort of role in Oliver's new world order." But actually, I just grinned stupidly. I still feel guilty for removing the poor boy from the safety of a hospital and totally confused that someone as hopelessly flawed as me could help to produce such a beautiful child.

"Aren't you clever?"

Competitive Dad Syndrome – Stage One

This was the first time I showed the symptoms of CDS – Competitive Dad Syndrome – a particularly serious illness of the mind that can affect any new father. It's hard to avoid, but there are ways – never use a video camera around your child, never involve your child in a sporting event, never dress your child in your favourite team's colours, never take your child to a public play park, or indeed any sort of public place.

As I've been guilty of all the above, I'm not well placed to advise on avoiding CDS, but I can offer some tips on controlling your behaviour around others. Rule one – introductions. When you introduce your baby to other people, they will almost certainly come out with 'Oh, he/she's beautiful'. If they're a new parent themselves (and they do tend to flock towards you) you should be aware that they're expecting a compliment in return.

Sometimes this can be tough, forcing you to reach deep into the recesses of your vocabulary to find a polite way to describe the gargoyle lying in their pram, but you must always say something, even if it's a distraction technique like 'he gets it from his mother', or 'look out for that bus'.

It's a British national characteristic to despise success that's easily worn, so if you want to keep the sympathy of well-wishers you'll add in something about how tough night-times are, or how he may look like an angel but he can be a demon. Try not to go too far the other way and let this turn into a desperate moan.

In short, be confident of your child's beauty and talent and don't rely on second hand praise to reassure you as a dad. I know that seems tough right now – but don't worry, we'll be coming back to it.

When we'd been to see our neighbours a week after their little girl was born, she was sleeping 12 hours a night and they were relaxed, confident and assured. It gave me so much confidence that I would cope with our own child. But now they are shadows of their former selves – she's stopped sleeping well and they're in a permanent trance. I don't know which version is our future, but I know which I'd rather.

We got Oliver inside, laid him down in his little carrycot and made ourselves a cup of tea. We sat and watched him for a while in silent wonder. Then I put the TV on. New parenthood in all its glory.

Chapter Two
The first night

"For the whole of our first night at home I just kept thinking 'what have I done, what have I done?'" P, dad of one.

What's happening?

Day two

Your baby — After a quiet start, the baby may now be finding its voice big time. Don't worry too much about all the crying at this early stage, there is a process of readjustment for this tiny being, fresh out of the cosy womb. If you spend some time holding your baby now, you might notice a couple of strange features. On the top of your baby's head, near the front, is a small diamond-shaped gap where the bones of the skull haven't knitted together yet. This is called the fontanelle and it is perfectly normal. It can take anything up to a year for the bones to form properly, but in the meantime it is perfectly safe. You can sometimes see the fontanelle pulse as your baby breathes. You might also notice that your baby's genitals are a bit swollen. This is also normal and everything will settle down after a few weeks.

Your partner – On coming home, your partner might actually start to relax a bit, but this can have its own impact. Her body is still getting used to the idea of no longer being pregnant, she is still bleeding a fair amount and her hormones are still playing havoc with her emotions. She may start to feel low and depressive – the so-called 'baby blues' (see chapter three for more information).

This afternoon and evening have been dominated by a series of small tasks that have taken hours of planning, lengthy execution and an eternity of clearing up. We've managed to get the nappy change down to something manageable – around half an hour – but it still feels like a manual dexterity task from The Krypton Factor.

Washing the baby is even more of a juggling act and feeding is a slow and frustrating process for mother and son. He's not taking well to the breast, so he's getting some expressed milk too. Everything seems so huge – the clothes we've bought for him, his bed, his pram. It's all too soon, he's not done yet and he needs to go back in for a few months.

Another thing that doesn't feel at all ready is our house. The whole place feels cold and harsh – the clay tiles on the floor are hazards in waiting, the big old stone fireplace is a potential nightmare and the stairs – well, don't even get me started on the stairs. For some reason I feel completely responsible for ensuring safety in the house. Everything has to be right but it clearly can't be, not unless I can find the energy to pad every surface and remove every danger. Babies are tough, babies are resourceful, babies are survival experts. That's right, keep repeating it, you lazy bastard.

Padded cell anyone?

Preparing your home for the baby

To the point. This is another area where the combined mantras of 'be prepared' and 'don't panic' hold true. There's not much point 'baby proofing' the whole house at this stage, as the little soul won't be up and about for months. When you do get as far as the crawling stage your priorities should be restricting access to hot surfaces, sharp edges and electricity. Until your baby is capable of responding to commands, this is essentially a process of shutting junior out of the kitchen and making fires/heaters/stoves inaccessible. You can buy plastic covers that go over power points and prevent the video recorder from becoming a post box for crayons. You won't need things like stair gates at any time in the first several months (although I've found they are a good way of keeping pets downstairs), but you will need to keep an eye out for anything that's at head-bumping level for the baby from the age of mobility (six months plus). That means putting protective corners on coffee tables and removing any low-level breakables.

The heat is on. Even if you can't clad the house in bubble wrap, you should still make some basic provisions for the return from hospital. Temperature is a big thing for newborns – as they aren't really any good at controlling their own. Make sure the rooms you're using for the baby have a decent background heat of around 18-21° C.

The right stuff. If you've bought a cot or crib don't expect to be using it straight away. Imagine you're a baby, wrenched from the cosy and comfortable womb – you're bound to be happier in tight spaces, so a padded Moses basket is a good first step. Move up to the crib or cot in a few weeks when the world doesn't seem like such a big and scary place. There needs to be a safe, level place for this in the bedroom, the nursery and probably the lounge because the baby won't always go to sleep where you want it to.

We saw this and thought of you. With the exception of nappies, clothes and the car seat, you don't really need anything else right now, though that won't stop some well meaning friend buying your day old child a 4x4 quad bike. If friends and family are pestering you for gift ideas and you're struggling to keep them at bay, go for the safe option of plain bodysuits and sleepsuits – you can never have too many of these, and they'll save you from having to do endless washing.

Eventually the time came to settle him down in his massive crib. We put a teddy in with him for company and sang him a song. He went off like a dream. It couldn't have been easier. But, by the time we'd got downstairs and finished slapping each other on the back, the hammering started – our new neighbour doing a spot of DIY at 10pm on a Sunday. Oliver woke and started to cry, Elle screamed in frustration. I clenched my fists and went next door to introduce myself.

I'm not an angry person, and I did manage to keep a lid on my obvious anger. But I don't think we'll be holidaying together for a while. The hammering stopped and I returned, breathing deeply.

Oliver hasn't been so easy to quieten. He's found every

excuse under the moon to stay awake all night. Our neighbour drove off about midnight – either to find somewhere quiet to sleep or to fetch his big brother with an even bigger hammer.

We've bravely tried to sit with Oliver in shifts, but I can't sleep knowing Elle's stuck with a crying child, and she feels the same. When all those knowing, cynical parents tell you that your baby's cries cut through you like a knife they're not kidding. It's impossible to ignore, and heartbreaking to hear.

At one stage I took him downstairs to give Elle a break and sat him in the swing that we bought him on a friend's advice. I started it rocking and playing its merry tune. This pushed Oliver to a new and unimagined level of misery. So he came out again and I cuddled him and sang to him and danced around the room until my feet were sore and my head was throbbing.

Scream test

How to survive the first night

Don't panic. To ensure that the planet stays populated, no-one tells you quite how awful it is to spend a night awake with your screaming child – which you'll probably be doing more in the first couple of weeks as a dad than at any other time.

The crying game. Crying is a baby's way to communicate. It doesn't always mean 'I am desperately ill', in fact it sometimes means 'I'm fed up' or 'I'm a bit peckish', but unlike the Eskimos, who have a variety of names for snow, the baby has just one name for everything – 'waaah'. The only way to stop a baby crying is to fix whatever's wrong and then calm the baby. The first part of this equation is easier to work out – basically you have a choice from the following: hungry, too hot or too cold, bored or lonely, windy or colicky, wet or dirty nappy, sleepy. Once you have correctly identified which of these is troubling the baby, you then have to distract the poor little mite until they forget that they were upset in the first place. If you're lucky, you'll have one of those babies that can be calmed by a mobile (hanging, not telephone), but the statistics suggest you're more likely to have a baby that will only be calmed by a lot of rocking, gentle, calming talk and a great deal of patience.

The longest night. It's almost impossible to explain the special combination of fear, frustration, guilt and regret that took over on that first
night – and to a lesser extent on many other nights over the first few
weeks. The worst part was feeling totally unable to calm Oliver – I was
really frightened that we'd created this new life and had no understanding of it, that he was going to be miserable for ever and we
weren't going to help.

Everyone's experience is different and most people find a way to cope
in the end. The only hope I can offer while you're watching the Open
University with the sound off in the small hours is that everything you
experience with babies is a phase, good or bad. Whatever's going
wrong will ultimately get better, whatever's going right will ultimately
go wrong. I don't know whether that's reassuring, but it makes perfect
sense in the middle of the night.

Get organised. Lack of sleep is a classic torture technique because
it is so incredibly effective. Unless you're one of those freakish,
lucky souls with a baby that sleeps, you are going to be really tested
over the coming weeks. When you're back at work, you might expect
to be let off some of the night-time chores, but even then you'll
have to do at least some of the after hours care or your partner will
go crazy.

Your best bet is to get a good strategy for dealing with an 'all-nighter' in place now, rather than after weeks of misery. It took us a long time to find a system that worked, but eventually we divided our night into three four hour sessions of 'baby watch'. One of us would take the first session (9pm-1am), the other would take the second (1-5am) and then the first person would return to duty for the final session (5-9am). We'd take it in turns each night.

The middle session is definitely the hardest as it's the most unnatural time to be awake. But whoever has to do that session gets the bonus of a decent eight hours sleep – the other person is only guaranteed four hours minimum, but you'll be surprised how well you can manage with very little sleep – just look at Margaret Thatcher (five hours a night). On second thoughts, don't.

As 4am approached, I lay down with him on the spare bed we'd made up in his nursery – our most brilliant idea. He was exhausted, cuddling into my crooked arm and fighting for a comfortable space to doze off. Sleep was impossible for me, I kept worrying that he would fall out of bed or that I'd roll over onto him. As the new day started to dawn around the edges of the blackout curtain, the worst thought in my mind was 'this is how life will be from now. The way I feel is never going to change, I'm simply going to get used to it'. It's just possible that we have made a truly terrible mistake.

There have been a few times in life when I've stayed awake all night – mainly when we've been going on holiday, and we're booked on a stupidly early flight. By the time the night has passed I'm usually in a trance, an empty shell heading for the hotel and complete collapse. Today is the first time in my life I've been through an all-nighter and still had to get up to face a long line of chores – and the first visit of the new grandparents.

I started with the basics. As people were coming to visit, clothes were needed. So I needed to get dressed. But this meant finding clothes and getting my legs and arms to behave. Too much to handle first off.

I went to the toilet, fortunately remembering to make it all the way to the bathroom first. Encouraged by this major achievement I tackled the stairs. Another success. Arriving in the lounge like an explorer fresh back from the North Pole, I noticed Elle had fed, changed, washed and clothed Oliver. I realised she must have secretly got some sleep while I wasn't looking. I decided to hold this against her for ever, and to go and make a cup of tea just for myself. And then I found that I'd walked into the cupboard under the stairs for some reason.

Oliver was making no secret of his desire to sleep. Apparently, he couldn't work out why we'd been so keen to keep him up all night, he was out cold the minute his head hit the mattress in his carrycot.

Which just left the pair of us, bleary eyed and snappy, sitting together and shivering over cups of tea. The miracle of parenthood in all its glory. Just a couple of days in, and Oliver already has us where he wants us. Elle's adapted to her new role as baby servant with her usual stiff upper lip – in fact she was well prepared for it, cooking and freezing an impressive collection of shepherd's pies and other easy cook delights. Thank God for her, otherwise we'd be starving as well as miserable and tired. Just to think, so called friends of mine have said that life will be back to normal soon – even sex life – right now I can't imagine having sex, I can't even summon up the strength to think about it. If I feel this exhausted after one night, I can't see it getting any better soon.

The contraception deception
Getting used to condoms again

Ok, so all that wonderful, spontaneous sex during pregnancy was great, but unless you want another blessed event nine months after the first one, you are going to need to be 'suited' when you do start having sex again. When this will be depends on you, and to a much greater extent, on your partner (see chapter four). But as soon as sex resumes you must use a condom or another form of contraceptive if you don't want to get her pregnant, even if you're one of the lucky ones and it's just days after giving birth.

While your partner's period may not return for a few months, she is still fertile, and a lot of people find themselves unexpectedly 'expecting' once again shortly after the dust has settled on pregnancy number one. If you really don't fancy the idea of wearing a condom once again, you may be able to persuade your partner to go for a cap or diaphragm – which can be used six weeks after pregnancy, or if your partner isn't breastfeeding she can go back on the pill from 21 days after pregnancy. But given the presence of the screaming bundle in the corner, you probably won't need too much persuading to take extra precautions for a while.

As for me, well I'm struggling. I'm never very good after a broken night's sleep, and my mood is made worse by the knowledge that this will just be the first night of many. But at least we had a brief period of calm as he slept and we waited for the grandparents and the return of the dogs.

Before long they arrived. The dogs rushed into the living room and sampled the strange new smells. One of the cats wandered up to them as if to whisper 'get out, run while you still can', but they were too focused on the deep breathing coming from the carrycot. We held them up for a quick look and a sniff as Elle's parents hung around in the background, desperate for their chance (to look, not to sniff).

And they looked. In fact they looked with just enough noise to stir him gently from his sleep. So then they got to have a cuddle, too. This is a trick I've observed in my mother with her other grandchildren – an ability to wake babies from 50 yards, but still leave them in beautiful moods so they cuddle snugly in her arms. There must be a granny aroma that's particularly attractive to children.

I admit I was worried about this first visit. I had a vision of long lectures about how cold/warm/tired/awake/hungry he was, but just like Oliver himself, they behaved very well. Elle and I both frowned when they tried to hold him and drink coffee at the same time and when they took too many photos, but otherwise it was a good first meeting with the outside world.

And, of course, they brought loads of presents which I spent many happy minutes opening and playing with. The tiredness suddenly went – maybe this 'being a dad' lark has its benefits after all. They didn't stay long as the midwife was due, but they got us to agree to another visit before the weekend. My parents are booked for mid-week, along with yet another midwife appointment. So much for time together as a family.

Man about the house

What to do with your paternity leave

Paternity leave is a strange time. At one end of the scale it's a two week break for men to learn fatherhood – like one of those intensive driving courses – and at the other it's a period in which you are expected to cook, clean, entertain and support. Neither situation is ideal, but as it's likely to be the best thing on offer for most working men, you need to make the most of the time – with a bit of forward planning you should be able to juggle between the extremes.

The return of the hired slave. This is a role that you might have hoped to leave behind in pregnancy. One cause of this problem may also be the solution – the gangs of visitors who show up at random expecting a glass of champagne and a finger buffet. Be mean – if people want to come and visit the new arrival tell them to bring their iron, or a casserole, or whatever they can offer that makes your life easier and gives you the chance to achieve the objective of spending time with your partner and child. It's either that or get your mother-in-law to move in for a fortnight. I thought not.

Controlling the relatives. Keeping family and friends in check, whether in the hospital or at home, will inevitably become one of your main roles in the first few days. They will behave like baby-crazed maniacs given the chance. It's your job to ensure that no visit lasts long enough to tire out your partner and child, that no-one hogs the baby or spends hours taking flash photos.

You'll also need to make it clear that there's no order of priority for visitors – all access should be requested through you, and you should make sure everyone who wants to see the new arrival gets to do so, and not just those who shout loudest or pester you.

It'll be your task to come up with food and drink for all these people and you can either go for the bring-your-own policy outlined above or provide as little as possible – which is another good way to stop them coming back for more.

Managing pets around babies. This is another type of shepherding activity, and it'll also be your task. Some people take a black and white view on pets and babies – scared by stories about suffocating cats and mauling dogs, they drag the pets straight off to the knackers' yard. This is a natural, overprotective fear and is particularly common in fathers, though it's a bit harsh, given the good work the pet has put in as a surrogate child over the years.

But there's no denying that a child's arrival changes the nature of your relationship with four legged friends. Animals will accept a new pack member without fuss as long as certain things are observed – get visitors to fuss dogs before they coo over the baby, don't try to train cats to keep out of the cot, just make it impossible for them to get in – perhaps by using a net – and try not to change walking and feeding routines for them.

If pets don't feel the impact of the new arrival too much, they're less likely to react to it by being aggressive or disruptive. That being said, even if the baby is accepted by your dog, it may be more likely to bark and growl at other dogs, passing motorists or falling leaves – it may think it's helping to protect the baby but this behaviour can move into all-out aggression against other animals and people if you're not careful.

Don't despair. Given the amount of practical assistance you'll be giving over this period, the amount of bonding time you'll get is probably minimal. Try not to be too down if your paternity leave isn't all you hoped. Apart from your normal leave entitlements, you also have the right to 13 weeks unpaid parental leave per child. This can be taken up until their 5th birthday. For more information visit the DTI website (**www.dti.gov.uk**).

Chapter Three
The first week

"Don't just hand over your child to an eager grandma – you're the dad and you are just as good at childcare as anybody else – if not better." G, dad of two

---

What's happening?

Week one

Your baby – Your baby has complete control of all their senses, albeit on a pretty limited scale. Your baby's eyes will focus on objects about 30cm away, so make sure you get up fairly close when you're chatting. Babies will react to bright lights, so tell the relations to keep their distance with flash cameras. After a couple of days babies often develop a yellow tinge to their skin and to the whites of their eyes. This is known as jaundice and relates to the fact that the liver is not completely developed. It usually fades within just a few days, but severe jaundice needs to be treated in the hospital. The midwife will keep a close eye on the baby's skin tone over the first week. The midwife will also prick your baby's heel with a needle to get a blood sample which is used to test for a range of diseases and conditions.

Your partner – She will probably be struggling to do anything other than attend to the baby's feeding needs right now, which means you'll have to do the chores (or get someone else to do them). The first week or so is a vital time for your partner's recovery and she needs a lot of sleep, so try to create the right environment for her to relax.

Our first meeting with the midwife since Oliver was born followed much the same pattern as the ante-natal visits. She spoke in smug, patronising tones to Elle, explaining how tough it was going to be to manage everything alone, while ignoring me completely. She did speak to me once, but only to ask when I'd be getting back to the office. I calmly explained for the ninetieth time that I worked from home and so wouldn't be going to any offices in the near future. She gave a strangled cough, as if choking back vomit at the idea of a father in the home full time. And that was that for this visit – still, at least it made me feel that I hadn't become completely invisible.

"So, Mrs M, we meet again."
Dealing with the midwife

In some ways, it was a comfort to see the midwife again, like meeting a familiar old enemy. But in other, more realistic ways, it was a pain in the arse to be reminded how useless I'm meant to be.

In pregnancy, her main concern was Elle. After the birth, her focus shifted to the baby. I didn't really get a look-in at any stage. It was OK during pregnancy, but not afterwards.

We'd always made it clear to her that we planned to share the child-care, but her attitude suggested we were making a big mistake. Given that Elle was tired and lost in her own thoughts in the days after the birth, the midwife should have been putting many of her comments and questions directly to me. That never happened, and it was a constant source of irritation.

From my survey of fathers I know that not all midwives are the same – in fact most are excellent – but a fairly big number seem stuck in a pattern of behaviour that's worked for them over many years. They need to change or be made to change if they're to be stopped from depressing another generation of fathers.

The midwife may have stayed exactly the same but there are major changes planned elsewhere in the household. After last night's disaster, we've decided to keep him in the carrycot where he's done most of his sleeping to date. It's wedged safely on to my desk at the end of our bed, so there's less of a distance to get to him when he cries. This means I can get up zombie-like and bring him to Elle in bed for a feed without ever waking up.

It also means that after months of careful planning and many hours of painting, shifting, grunting and swearing, the nursery I created is now empty. I have a secret desire to move myself back in and get back my former study – especially as my current working area is now filled by a sleeping child.

We've also put away the special baby sleeping bag we bought for him, preferring to stick with a blanket for now. We're pretty sure he'll be chilled out by the sounds of our breathing and might even get a decent night's sleep.

. . .

Another disaster. Well, not completely – the first night of the new plan was OK and we all got some rest. On the second night Oliver got a decent amount of sleep, but I was awake almost all night again. Part of it was down to the feeling of knowing he was going to wake eventually, so I was on edge waiting for it to happen. With Elle still pretty exhausted and in need of some decent sleep, I felt it was my duty to get up whenever possible.

By far the biggest worry on my mind was the blanket. Was it too tight, too thin, too thick, was he going to worm his way beneath it and suffocate? Every time he settled into a calm, deep sleep I strained to hear his breathing. I kept getting up all the time to check, twice waking him.

In pregnancy, my permanent fears were about miscarriage or stillbirth, and now, since the birth, I have become obsessed with cot death. My fears have a similar root – that something terrible could happen to someone I love and I may not be able to stop it. I'm in that dangerous area between knowledge and ignorance where I understand the basic ways to limit cot death, but these still don't give me the guarantees that would make me comfortable.

While I've read everything I can find on the subject over the last couple of days, I don't feel I can talk about it. It's not fair to burden Elle with my fears. Though I'm fairly sure she has the same things going through her mind, they may not be keeping her awake at night and I'd rather it stayed that way. The philosophical attitude would be that if nothing can be done, there's nothing to worry about. But a quick search of blockbuster movie history shows that philosophers never saved the Earth from asteroid attack, so I'm happier doing something in the belief that I can say I tried. I just wish that I could worry in my sleep.

Thinking the unthinkable

Guarding against cot death

Cot death, or Sudden Infant Death Syndrome (SIDS), is a horrible thought, but it is important to know something about it so you can put the risks into perspective. There's something like a one-in-two thousand chance that your baby may be the victim of cot death. Advances have been made in finding the causes of this mysterious killer, and while it is still broadly an unknown area, there is hope that the battle is slowly being won.

Reducing the risk. There's a variety of ways to cut the risk of cot death. I've already touched on the importance of keeping room temperature under control so that it's never too hot or too cold in the baby's room. Never use loose bed clothes like a duvet with a baby – better to use a tucked-in blanket or a baby sleeping bag. If you're using a blanket, make sure the baby's feet are close to the bottom end of the cot, so they can't wriggle down any further. Newborn babies should always be laid on their backs. Smoking is another major factor – never smoke in a room that the baby will sleep in – in fact never smoke anywhere near a baby in any event. Other rules are a bit less useful – never handle a baby when you're extremely tired, for example. Not always easy to manage that one. It translates as 'don't snuggle up under your warm duvet with the baby'.

A lot of this may be common sense, but it clashes with a lot of previous thinking – look through a baby care book from the 1970s or 80s and you'll find contrary advice, so don't be tempted to listen to your parents on this one.

Talking helps. It can be hard to deal with something so horrific knowing that sometimes it just happens and you can do nothing about it, but it is something you should talk over with your partner – you can be fairly sure she's having the same fears and by talking them through you're a step closer to coping with the issue in the unlikely and unfortunate event it becomes a reality. For extra support, the Foundation for the Study of Infant Deaths has an excellent website (sids.org.uk) with more detailed information.

• • •

Today gave us something else to worry about – the return of the midwife. Seeing her every couple of days is going to be tough, especially if today's show is anything to go by.

On the plus side she remembered to bring the scales. She put Oliver on and studied the display with a frown on her face. We were both watching her closely and something was definitely wrong. She took him off then put him back again.

"Something the matter?" I said, nervously. You could say that. According to the scales, Oliver has lost a pound and a half in the five days since he was born. The midwife said that while many babies lose some weight after birth, few lose it at such a rapid speed. In fact, she said, she'd only ever known one other baby lose weight at such a rate.

"And what happened to that baby?" we both asked.

"Oh it died," she said. "But try not to worry."

Our jaws dropped and we sat in stunned silence as she sipped her coffee, safe in the knowledge that she'd managed to scare the living shit out of us. As Elle was about to speak there was a knock at the front door – it was my parents, with their arms full of presents. I took one look at Elle and then stood up, grabbed my coat and hurried them away from the door, down the path and back along the road. As we walked away I tried to explain what was going on but, to be honest, I didn't have a clue myself.

On the one hand, the midwife seems to think that Oliver is a healthy and happy baby, albeit one who isn't taking well to breast feeding. But on the other hand she seems worried that his weight has dropped so much. She even suggested that his generally quiet and relaxed manner is possibly down to 'lethargy'.

To me, walking in a daze in the autumn sunshine with my confused parents, it felt like we'd been accused of failing to care for our baby – possibly with fatal results.

I didn't know what to say to my mum and dad, they'd come to meet their new grandson and were met with a scene of such emotional chaos they must have genuinely wondered how he'd made it this far. I couldn't even imagine what Elle was going through at home, still trapped with the Midwife of Doom.

Eventually the midwife drove past with a beep of the horn and a cheery wave. When we got home Elle was in tears. Right then I wanted my parents to go, and if they hadn't just driven for four hours to get to us, I might have asked them to. It would have been a mistake, left to ourselves we'd have worked each other into a state of total misery. Instead we had to focus on the familiar routine of tea and cakes, on smiling as the proud grandparents held our son for the first time, even though my gut instinct was to snatch him away and never let go.

They also offered a degree of logic to ease our fears over the midwife's visit. They felt certain that the mystery of the disappearing pound and a half lay in a misread weigh-in at the hospital. He was only weighed once during his stay, so it was possible his birth weight was written down wrong. We like this theory, even though neither of us really believes it. It's certainly better than the awful alternative.

Aside of the fact that today has left us feeling as emotionally knackered as we are physically exhausted, the biggest impact has been on feeding. What started out as a minor feud has become a full scale war, and we're determined there'll be no casualties on either side.

I can see why so many women give up breastfeeding early on. The genuine belief that it is the best form of feeding for a baby is clear to anyone who reads the facts. But no-one takes time to explain the real frustration felt by both parents when their child can't master the essential skill necessary for its own survival.

Elle wants to stick with breastfeeding, which, according to the midwife, means not using bottles as the rubber teats get the baby confused. The baby isn't the only one. I'm pretty mixed up as to how we are expected to increase his body weight but not resort to bottle feeding. It's like a sick joke.

I'm powerless – unable to feed him myself and unwilling to withdraw my support for Elle's decision to breastfeed him. All I do is stand around looking and feeling like a spare part once more. I thought that feeling would go away after pregnancy, that once Oliver was born there was nothing that I couldn't do as well as Elle. I was wrong.

•   •   •

Today Oliver is one week old. If every other week of his life is like this first one, I'll be either mad or dead within a year. If pregnancy was like a rollercoaster, the week since my son's birth has been like one of those fairground rides where you're spun around and around until you pass out and are then dropped a hundred metres into a pool of alligators. What? – There's no such ride? They should invent one, and call it The Baby.

Actually, the baby isn't the problem here. He's the only one of us who's still coping with life. He's drinking expressed milk from a cup – the only way we can get him fed and not stuck on the bottle. The one big advantage of this is I can now help out with the feeds, which stops me fretting on the sidelines.

The right start

Helping her through feeding

While most fathers I surveyed were happy with the level of involvement they had with their baby in the first few weeks, a fair number would have liked to do more.

Breast envy. The one area that's obviously a closed book to new dads is breastfeeding. That doesn't matter if all is well and the baby's feeding happily, but if things aren't going well it can be extremely frustrating to be on the sidelines and unable to help. You have another balancing act on your hands – while you want to keep your baby healthy, now is not the time to be the 'master of your house' and insist the baby goes on to formula milk.

Breastfeeding is, I'm told, a sometimes tough and sometimes painful process, but it's the best method of feeding by far. Your partner has this fact rammed down her throat at every opportunity by the hospital, midwives and heath visitors and the pressure can be huge. So if it's not working out and she makes the tough decision to give up breastfeeding, she deserves total support, not a guilt-trip.

Express delivery. In this event, expressing milk into bottles is a good stepping stone between breast milk and formula milk – the baby still gets all the nutrients and you get to help out with the feeding (and bonding) process. Your partner can either express milk by hand, which can be quite a slow process, or she can use a breast pump (manual or automatic) which looks like a torture device left over from the Spanish Inquisition but is actually closely allied to the pumps used to milk cows – note: drawing comparisons here may not earn you any bonus points with your partner, though it may earn you a rare opportunity to sleep on the lawn. Once the milk has been expressed, it can be stored for up to a day in the fridge.

Feeding frenzy. Feeding the baby yourself is a great experience, and is about as close as you can get to your baby. It's a great help at night and on those odd occasions when your partner can actually get herself out of the house. You'll need to warm the milk, either using one of those slightly fiddly milk warmers that looked like a good idea in the shop or the traditional method of putting the bottle in hot water. Heating milk in the microwave is not recommended, as microwaves tend to heat things unevenly, creating 'hotspots' of extreme heat. But in an emergency, a quick zap in the microwave should be followed by a really good shake to ensure the heat is evenly distributed. Even then, you should test the temperature of the milk by shaking a little dab on to an area such as the inside of your wrist. Don't try to feed the baby milk that's too hot or cold – remember you are trying to recreate 'breast conditions' and those puppies are quite warm, so gentle heat is best.

Trick or teat. The actual feed isn't too much of a challenge, though there's a bit of a knack here, too. Be sure to tilt the bottle sufficiently to fill the whole teat (the plastic nipple on the end) with milk. If there's any air in the teat, the baby will suck that down and you'll be burping it until Tuesday. Don't worry if the baby doesn't drink all the milk in one go – and don't be tempted to chant 'down in one, down in one, down in one,' as they are gulping away. Instead, if the little soul is struggling, break off, give junior a cuddle and a back rub and inevitably you'll get a deep, satisfying belch. You may also get a load of backed-up milk for your trouble, so don't do a feed wearing your best clothes.

All the worry over his weight loss was the final straw for sleep. We've both given up, and lie awake wanting to talk but not being able to for fear of waking him or coming up with new worries. We've almost run out of our supplies of frozen ready meals and I'm in no mood to cook or make trips to the supermarket.

On the rare occasions that we have actually got dressed our clothes have been covered with burped up milk and they now sit in a menacing pile in the corner of the bedroom waiting for one of us to crack and actually attempt the washing.

And, as there's a 'y' in the day, there must also be a visit from family. This time it's the return visit of the parents-in-law accompanied by Elle's sister. She doesn't have a lot of experience handling babies and she was a bit nervous holding him at first. Elle and I didn't want to step in, but her parents got stuck in with criticism, instructions and advice.

I hadn't really thought much about this, but I guess they also have to do some readjusting in their new role. In truth, I don't like to think of anyone beyond Elle and I having a stake in Oliver's existence, but that's a selfish attitude which comes from a desire to protect him.

I know that I've got to get better at sharing him. But not just yet. We went for a walk to give Elle a couple of hours rest – I pushed the pram and gave the dogs to the grandparents.

Even then, right at the start of our walk, I could see the steely gleam in my mother-in-law's eye. She wanted that pram, and she was going to do all that she could to get it. The dogs were allowed to weave around my legs as a trip hazard. The minute we reached any slight hill a third hand would appear alongside mine 'to help out on the slope'.

Once she'd got the feel of that handle under her fingers she was focused – it must have taken great will power not to shoulder barge me from the pavement and take her place as the rightful pusher.

I knew my time was short, so as we turned for home, I decided to show off for a while, removing one hand from the pram.

I honestly believe the right to push a pram one-handed is a father's most important privilege. It's often mistaken as a sign of embarrassment or discomfort, but in truth it's the complete opposite – it's a bit like driving one handed, technically suspect, but carried out with the air of total confidence that suggests man and machine in complete harmony. I've practised it during the short trips we've made to walk the dogs on the patch of grass near our house, and have now developed it to the level of art form. I've even begun to make 'brrm-brrm' noises as I push.

This time, however, the one handed push was a fatal error of judgement. It gave mother-in-law the space to make a two handed lunge for the pram. I then had to make it very clear I was going to let her push anyway, and was sure to criticise her driving all the way home. Oliver slept throughout – or at least he kept his eyes firmly shut.

He sleeps a lot in the pram; I guess the gentle rhythm of being wheeled through ditches and across ploughed fields relaxes him. It can be pretty annoying, given that we only take him out for dog walks on the off-chance that the neighbours will see us and rush over to say how clever we are to have produced a beautiful child. What might previously have been a five minute dash has become a half hour stroll, soaking up the congratulations of the neighbourhood and dragging our feet in the vain hope that more people will come out to see us.

Despite my protests before, during and after the visit, it's been good to have family over again. Elle enjoyed the break, I enjoyed the fights and they all agreed totally with our dodgy diagnosis that the hospital/midwife/scales must be wrong as Oliver is a healthy, happy and very bright baby.

Tomorrow we'll discover whether he's putting on weight as the midwife returns with the dreaded scales. She's the last person I want to see, but I'm very keen to erase her miserable outlook.

Swings and roundabouts

Handling the post-birth blues

Putting aside the fact that you'll both be extremely tired and working pretty much on autopilot, you might also notice a big dip in your partner's mood in the days after the birth. This can sometimes be mistaken for post-natal depression (see Information Panel in chapter five). In fact it's nowhere near as serious, and rarely lasts longer than a couple of days.

It's most likely to be down to a hormone surge which effectively overwhelms your partner with tiredness and emotion – leaving her weepy or exhausted. Watch out for it, because it's your job to give her the confidence to get through this particular trough, ensuring it doesn't lead to more serious and long term problems.

One great way to beat the blues is to get some personal space. Many new parents fall into a trap of doubling up on childcare, particularly when they're tired. There were many times when one of us could have been doing something else – reading a book, getting some sleep, doing the shopping – but out of instinct we sat together waiting for Oliver's next instruction. Looking back, this was a terrible waste of precious personal time. Though it's early days, you should try to set a routine at home which allows each of you some space from the baby – even if it's just for a couple of hours at a time.

Tonight we celebrate his first seven days. I guess if no other positive has emerged from the worry over his weight, it has started to bond us as a family. We've been so low this week there were times when I admit I've suspected or even blamed Elle for Oliver's problems. I've no idea why as it's not based on any rational ideas – I guess I've just wanted to lash out, blame someone and ease my guilt. It's not something I'm proud of.

Despite all the fears we've tried to stay positive and focused – though it would be pretty easy to get down over the lack of sleep, the seemingly endless list of chores and the fact that life is one big routine, without excitement or change – a mechanical process of feeding, cleaning, cuddling, burping and washing. And there's the baby to think of too.

Chapter Four
The first month

"Don't be swayed by outside influences – do it your way. Despite other opinions our son was in his cot after three days and was sleeping through the night by four weeks." R, dad of one.

What's happening?
Month one

Your baby – After a fairly nerve-wracking start to life, your baby is probably starting to strengthen, particularly in the neck muscles, so you won't have to deal with quite such a wobbly head. Another new feature is your baby's smile – for some weeks you've probably been trying to spot this milestone, only to have elderly relatives inform you delightedly that 'it's just wind'. Well now it might actually be a smile. Or wind.

Your partner – Things should be getting easier for your partner now. The exhaustion and physical strain of pregnancy will be fading into memory, and hopefully the emotional lows of baby blues will have passed as well. Her body will be returning to normal too, and with a sensible diet and a bit of gentle exercise she should be able to get her pre-pregnancy figure back sooner rather than later.

I'm a big fan of the midwife. No, not that one, but the wonderful woman who came out to see us for the first time today and told us that Oliver's gained a few ounces and is a perfectly healthy baby. She couldn't understand what all the fuss has been about. We can breathe again.

I feel happy we've been proved right, that there was probably some mistake along the way and he's doing fine. But I also feel angry that our first week as a family was clouded by so much unnecessary fear. Given that I can't do a thing about it, this is probably one area where the philosopher does save the day – time to move on.

We planned an adventure to celebrate our good news. We decided to head out on the first official Giles family outing – a 15 mile round trip in the car with a stop for lunch in the middle. It's a safe distance, not so far that we can't rush home in an emergency, not so close that we'll be recognised if Oliver screams blue murder.

With the destination agreed, we began the simple process known as 'getting ready' around midday. It works something like this: We feed him, change him and dress him. Then we realise we should take a change of clothes, nappies and wipes. Make it a couple of nappies to be on the safe side. But then there ought to be a couple of changes of clothes, just in case. I take the pram to pieces and place it in the car boot. What about toys? Which toys will he need? We hunt around for toys that go with a 15 mile round trip with lunch in the middle. We find his outdoor outfit and his in-car outfit. We spend five minutes discussing the pros and cons of the pram and decide against. I unload it and put it back together again.

By now he needs another change and is closing fast on another feed. Oliver is removed from his going-out clothes, fed and changed. He is dressed again. I go out to warm up the car, Elle follows with Oliver and I return to bring up the rear with a shed load of baby products. With everything finally crammed into the car we're ready for the off. It's just after 3pm.

It will get better – we will get better. We have to, unless we want to eat off the afternoon tea menu for the rest of our lives. Having a baby in tow requires an incredible amount of planning, and given that I'm known to lock us out of the house and/or forget my wallet on a regular basis, I have a long way to go to get organised.

Oliver didn't like the car very much. I think he'd been a bit overwhelmed by his 'prison break' from the hospital to notice the first journey, but he took against this one from the start. We sang to him and whispered calmly, I tried desperately to remember the nursery rhymes of my childhood – without the rude lyrics of my teenage years.

It wasn't much fun, but soon we arrived at our 'lunch' destination, walked into the town centre, had a coffee and a cake and Oliver started to get used to the idea of being out in public. He was soaking up the sights, sounds and smells of a new atmosphere.

Walking back to the car we were stopped by a couple of old ladies wanting to take a look at Oliver.

"Oh," they sighed. "How old?" they chorused, sounding like a couple of Albert Steptoe impersonators.

Elle smiled the kind smile she reserves for the old people who flock around her like, well, like old people. "Just a week," she said.

One of them nearly fainted, the other took a step back into the road and narrowly avoided being flattened by a Norbert Dentressangle lorry. When they'd collected themselves, one turned to the other and said: "They do, though, these days." They wandered on, shaking their heads in amazement.

I assume they meant it was too soon for Oliver to be out of hospital, or for Elle to be back on her feet. They come from a generation where mother and child would stay in quarantine until the infant was old enough to go up his first chimney.

With my usual air of self-involvement, I take great offence at any hint that my wife and child are in any danger being out in public just a week after the birth. Anyway it took so much effort to get them there, I'm not going to suddenly retreat back indoors on the orders of a pair of old crones.

•   •   •

Actually, over the last week we've gone to the opposite extreme, finding any old excuse to venture out – partly to get Oliver more familiar with the car and partly to escape from the piles of washing, rubbish and other sinister crap that currently fill our house.

The game of the name

Registering the birth

One of our earliest trips out was to the register office where we officially declared Oliver's existence and his name. In some areas this process can be done at the hospital, as a kindly visiting registrar will record all the birth details before you have the chance to f orget them.

You must register the birth within 42 days, and if you want both your names to appear on the register you must both attend the registration or the absent partner must submit their details on a form available from the General Register Office. You don't need any other paperwork.

It's a touching and important part of the process of becoming a parent that also has a fairly sober and lasting impact on your child's life. Although it's not your last chance to go back on the decision to name your child after the Premiership title winning squad, it does formalise your baby's existence.

In another major step towards normality, we went to the supermarket today. Things started badly as yet another pair of crones swooped on us in the car park, craning their wobbly necks to see him in his car seat. One of them was smoking and I gave her a filthy look. She continued to gawp and puff away regardless, so I edged him slowly away under the laughable pretext of being in a hurry.

There must have been some special offer on baby products at the store today, because it was packed to the rafters with tiny, screaming bundles and their ill-tempered parents. The ratio of mothers to fathers was unexpectedly low, about four to one I reckon. That either means a lot of blokes willingly take time out of their busy schedules to go shopping, or more likely they are forced to tag along if they want to have something to eat for the rest of the week.

None of the lone parents with children were actually taking things off the shelves. Instead they were locked in negotiations over which toys/sweets/biscuits/crisps would be enough to get everyone out of the place alive.

By studying the behaviour of other fathers I could see I was meant to be the fetcher-carrier, picking up products under instruction from Elle, while she pushed the trolley and kept Oliver happy. I wasn't doing my job very well because I was too busy staring at other people's babies.

I may be a bit biased, but other people's babies are hideous. Some of them border on the freakish – big jowly beasts that look like they've been drawn by a cartoonist with the shakes, tiny purple babies that are like those California Prunes from the 1980s adverts, strangely proportioned babies that look as if they have Mr Potato Head's features stuck on a Jersey Royal.

Some of them were so frightening I wanted to throw a fire blanket over them. I'm particularly upset by completely bald babies – it feels as if their flawless heads are going to suddenly spin around 360 degrees.

While I've got over any fears I may have had about handling Oliver, I know that I'm still a long way from liking babies in general. I dread the moment when somebody asks me to hold theirs, or even worse, compliment them on producing something that looks likes it's been made out of modelling clay and then left too near a heater.

"You must be very...scared?"

Competitive Dad Syndrome (CDS) Stage Two –

other people's babies

When you become a new dad there is a general assumption that you will now automatically like all babies. This didn't work for me, or for friends who still find themselves yawning whenever they meet baby bores at parties.

Instead, I'd say that I found other people's babies compelling – not just in their frequently odd features, but in manner, even their cries and laughter were different from Oliver's and that was strange and interesting. I found myself comparing his features to those of other children. This involved a lot of obvious gawping on my part and furious jabs in the ribs from Elle. I never got over the feeling that other children are strange and never have – children's parties are always a major flashpoint, as if someone has assembled an identity parade of hideousness and bad behaviour.

Of course we all favour our own child, there's a familiarity in the features and manner that is both attractive and comforting. Making endless comparisons might be a bit obsessive, but it is part of the natural process of measuring your child against others.

It's a pretty negative trait, but everyone does it — and it does tend to get worse (see CDS Stage Three). What's important is that you don't start to take your own hopelessly biased propaganda too seriously. Yes your child is wonderful, no that fact doesn't need to be broadcast from the rooftops.

* * *

Since Oliver's successful weigh-in, we've been getting fairly cocky about midwife visits. They won't give us a clear time slot for their appearances, so we do our best to be around, but we keep missing them. We get back from a walk to discover short, angry notes asking whether everything's OK, and telling us to reschedule. I guess the little bit of resentment that still lingers over the weight issue has made us question the point of these frequent visits.

Hopefully, the next appointment will be the last. A midwife is coming to sign us off and pass the baton of care to a health visitor. This slightly less starched version of the midwife will continue to check weight, offer advice on care and well-being and generally make sure all is well over the coming few weeks.

I'm particularly keen to ensure the handover goes smoothly. If the midwife thinks we need more time under her care, we won't get signed off. This has built the stress surrounding the appointment to the level of an examination or job interview. It's the first real chance for an outside observer to judge us as parents.

If all goes well, I can launch a charm offensive on the health visitor and form a better relationship than the one I currently suffer with the midwives. If it goes badly, we're stuck with the midwives and the feeling that we're failing as parents.

• • •

Well, we made it through. Although it actually turns out there's no 'we' in sign-off. This part of the process was focused totally on Elle's physical well-being. It was fitting that I was totally redundant in this final session of midwife care. Yet again she stressed bossily that Elle shouldn't be lifting heavy objects and driving. Yet again Elle pointed to me and said that I was doing those things. Yet again the midwife struggled to bring her eyes to meet mine.

We live in different worlds – after months I understand that, I just don't appreciate it.

The health visitor showed up the next day, just to introduce herself and check out the quality of our chocolate biscuits. I made a special effort, even combing my hair for the occasion, and it seemed to do the trick. She was much more relaxed than the midwives, she wasn't in uniform for a start and didn't have that brusque, bustling manner that all midwives use. I'd go so far as to say she was chilled out.

She listened to our moans with the patience of a deaf priest and then told us how delighted she was that we were planning to share childcare. This was care on a totally new scale. I warmed to her immediately.

Same shit, different badge?

Getting to know the health visitor

Health visitors, like midwives, vary enormously from person to person. Some are traditionalists who'll speak to your partner in the third person as 'mum' all the time – e.g. 'And how's mum sleeping?' – and won't give you the time of day, some are very PC and will urge you to perform Guatemalan paternity rites while embroidering a quilt. Most are somewhere in between.

They differ from midwives in the sense that they exist mainly for the baby's benefit – they are the calm after sales service while the midwives are on the stressful factory floor. In my experience, health visitors are better prepared than midwives for dealing with parents rather than just mothers – ours was very supportive of plans to share childcare, and was very open and frank with us both. This immediately helped to make her more relevant and sympathetic to me as a father.

Even if you don't have the time, inclination or opportunity to see much of her, it's worth attending at least one appointment – this person will become fairly important in your partner's life over the next few weeks and months and it's worth introducing yourself to understand where she's coming from.

Depending on the level of help and support your partner feels she needs, the health visitor may stop visiting after three months or so, or she may make regular calls throughout the first year. Visits from the heath visitor are not like social services check-ups, they are no indication that you are failing in your duties as parents, instead it is just an opportunity to get first-hand expert guidance from someone who can genuinely say she's seen it all before.

After boasting about our thoroughly modern parenting plans, I've actually started to give them some serious thought. These first couple of weeks have been totally absorbed by childcare. Every moment we're not spending with Oliver we are using to catch up on our sleep.

I've not read a book or looked at a newspaper – even my endless scanning of Teletext for news on my football team has scaled back to a manageable couple of hours a day.

How the hell am I going to squeeze some work into this full routine? As a rule, I like to taunt my office-going friends about their commute, dress code and the million distractions that keep them from doing any work in their workplace, but now I can see that leaving the house every day would have its advantages.

One mate of mine has only just gone back to work after taking some leave for his first child's birth. I spoke to him about the joys of getting a break from the nappies and the burp cloths.

"It's not as great as it sounds," he said. "You think you're getting back to normality, but two things hit you. First, you realise exactly how short of sleep you are. You've only got to fall asleep in a meeting or accidentally call your boss 'darling' for the cracks to show.

"Secondly – and this is the worst part – every single person in the office wants to know exactly what's going on at home. It's not just the women, all the fathers come out of the woodwork and start to reminisce. So you're forever discussing the things you're trying to get some space from. Then the advice starts, and the offers start to flood in – 'we've got a trike we don't need, do you want it?' You're in an impossible situation, if you try to get on with your work, you're seen as cold-hearted. If you give in to all the interest, you'll never get a thing done."

Maybe I am better off at home. I have to come up with a way of finding the energy and space to start working again. The most important thing is not to stress – Elle's maternity leave package is quite good, so we're not going to need extra cash until she goes back part time in the new year. That's at least three months away. And I deserve a holiday after all I've been through.

Money, life and other problems

Managing the work/life balance

Unless you're the main carer, a home worker or very rich, you'll probably have returned to work by now. Aside of the changes to the office dynamic mentioned above, this will also affect your relationships at home, and it will prompt you to start thinking abut life's other big worry – money.

Cash flow problems. The main problem is that all the cash seems to be flowing in one direction – straight from your savings into the pockets of the nappy and baby toy manufacturers. But to ease the burden of the baby there are some possibilities open to you. One of the benefits of the registration process (see above) is not just the free certificate but also the fact that it's the first step to claiming child benefit, which all parents are entitled to regardless of income – you have to apply for it, and you'll need to send a form and the birth certificate to the Inland Revenue to qualify. This should also trigger payment of the Government's Child Trust Fund voucher. Other benefits, including the Sure Start Maternity Grant, are based on earnings – for the latest information check out the Inland Revenue website (www.hmrc.gov.uk).

Your partner and baby should also be benefiting from free NHS prescriptions for the next year, and she can even get dentistry work done for free – so even if her need isn't desperate, it's worth getting out there and taking advantage while it's available.

Setting up savings. The arrival of your child may be the perfect time to start thinking about putting some money away for their future, or at least to pay the bills when they write off your car at the age of 18. There's a range of options available to you depending on the level of risk you are prepared to take and how quickly you need to access the savings. One of the best medium-term savings accounts is a cash ISA, in which you can save a few thousand pounds each year completely tax free. If you're just looking for somewhere to squirrel away birthday and Christmas money, most banks offer children's savings accounts with excellent rates of interest. One great advantage of having some savings (particularly if they aren't instant access) is that you feel more secure without having the temptation to rush out and spend the money on a huge treat for your wonderful child, or your stressed wife, or you.

Where there's a will. While you're thinking about the financial side of your child's upbringing, it may be worth organising the legal side too. If you don't have a will, it is vital you make one now and that you consider the unpleasant possibility of what will happen to your money and your child if you and your partner die. You should decide who you would choose to act as your child's legal guardian in this event and enshrine this in a legal document as well.

Home life. There's likely to be a marked increase in stress surrounding night-time – you need your sleep to function the next day, your partner needs hers to cope with the baby. You can both make good cases – just because yours involves earning money there's no need to come over all caveman about it, you need to come up with a compromise.

Give her a break. There's other stresses – whether or not office life returns to normal for you, it is time out of the house and away from the routine of baby care. You need to ensure your partner has some time off planned, to break her routine with the baby – maybe the occasional afternoon off, or night out with friends – something that will help her feel that life isn't moving on without her.

Weekends are another potential problem, as they were once your time to relax after a busy week, but will now be filled with the many jobs that are impossible to manage in the week. Your partner has the upper hand here – your work is just five days a week, hers is seven, so you've got to bend on the weekend time. At least it's good for bonding – you'll be surprised at just how long Sky Sports News can hold the interest of a three week old baby.

• • •

Work isn't the only thing we've been putting off over the last few weeks. Our sex life was put on hold after about 34 weeks of pregnancy and it's stayed that way. Part of me (i.e. the business end) really wants it to start again. But another part of me (the brain) worries that I'll get Elle pregnant again, that I'll hurt her, that I'll appear selfish, that we'll wake the baby or that she just won't fancy me any more. That's just one – albeit nagging – pro against a whole load of cons.

I don't know whether any of those cons would actually happen, but if I try to initiate sex, or even a conversation about sex, I'm making a big statement which my sleep starved, anxious wife might not be terribly keen to hear. It'll sort itself out, given time. For once the brain wins the battle.

"Not tonight dear, I've got a baby"
Sex after birth

If, during pregnancy, you managed to keep your sex life strong, communicate all your fears and constantly reassure and satisfy your partner, move on to the next section. This is for all the men who found sex a bit of a challenge during pregnancy, and who are expecting an equally awkward time in the first few weeks and months of fatherhood.

There are two questions to ask about sex after birth – when can we? and when should we? Let's take a look at them both:

When can we? First things first – you can start having sex as soon as your partner feels comfortable enough to do so, which might be after a few weeks or maybe a couple of months. Don't assume this is some kind of rejection – it's just down to the trauma experienced by your partner's body in labour.

When should we? On to the second question – if your partner still doesn't seem ready for sex after a few weeks have passed, how do you get her to talk about the subject? This depends a lot on how your partner is coping with the baby – that's going to be the first thing on her mind, and if it's a struggle she probably won't thank you for wanting to get down and dirty with you. There's also a chance that she isn't feeling particularly sexy or attractive. If that's the case, it is down to you to make sure she knows you find her every bit as gorgeous as before.

Not up to it? The above point assumes that you want sex and she doesn't, but the reverse may also be true. Some men do experience a loss of drive after the birth, particularly if they've watched the whole contortion unfold and now feel slightly odd about their partner's private parts. There's nothing wrong with feeling a bit unsure about sex, but you need to air your feelings so that you can get beyond this.

Take it easy. We all know that sex isn't just about making babies, it's also a big part of a loving and supportive relationship, and that might be just what your partner needs while she's low. She might be glad to get out of being the mother and back into the role of lover for a while. It's a matter of judgement on your part, but it's better to talk it over in a non-pressurised environment than to stay quiet and turn it into an issue.

Find a space. Coming up with the right environment for sex can be tough – I'd recommend taking the baby out of the bedroom just for a while, going crazy and getting down to it in another room (remember the wild days of living room sex or kitchen quickies?) or if the baby's bottle feeding at night, get some trusted grandparents to stay over and take yourselves off to a hotel.

Left hand down a bit. On the practical front, what you do in bed may be linked to your partner's experience in labour and to her feeding regime. Some women have slight tears to the tissue around the vagina in labour, some have to be cut deliberately (known as a episiotomy) to get the baby out. These cuts are usually stitched and heal within weeks, but the area might be especially tender for a bit. Be gentle around Caesarean scars, and don't expect your post-op partner to be as lithe as a gymnast. Don't be surprised if it's a bit harder to get her 'lubricated' as well, some women find that birth makes their vagina a little drier than before, so initially you might want to consider using some lubricating jelly.

Up top, breastfeeding women aren't likely to be too fussed about having their nipples chewed by an enthusiastic lover. Nipples might be especially sensitive and ones that have a baby clamped to them for the best part of the day can be sore and cracked. So proceed with a bit more caution, at least in the early weeks and months.

Keep yourself to yourself. As with the later stages of pregnancy, you're likely to have a stronger sex drive than your partner's battered body can cope with, so it's up to you to ensure you relieve the pressure without making her life a misery. Masturbation will ease the frustration without making you public enemy number one.

Another fairly good reason to believe that sex isn't the first thing on Elle's mind is the mild pain she's still getting from her damaged pelvis. We've had to go back to the hospital to meet with the physiotherapist. It's the first time Oliver's been back to the dreaded place, and if I wasn't acting as official driver I wouldn't have brought him this time. Given the high volume of sick people associated with the hospital, I reckon it's the last place to take a new-born. I kept him clutched tight to my chest to ensure no killer bugs could sneak past my defences.

We weren't there for long, thank goodness, and the physio seemed happy with Elle's progress. Almost as important was the way she poured praise on Oliver's perfect behaviour. This is a great bonus of being a dad – not only was he well behaved, he was well behaved in my care, which reflects back onto me. It's a win-win situation.

This explains why so many fathers live their lives through their children – if I can turn him into a halfway decent left arm spinner or a premier league striker think how great I'll feel every time he mops up the Australian tail or hits a cup final hat-trick. He succeeds, I succeed. Oh yes, I get the idea of this fatherhood business.

In the waiting room there was a woman about to have a huge, hideous boil removed. No wait, it was a baby. In fact I can safely say it was the ugliest baby I've ever seen. I suspect she was bringing it back to ask for a refund. It was like an identikit of all the horrible features from the supermarket babies – purple face, wrinkled skin, domed head, angry whine. Elle jabbed me firmly in the ribs – I was copying its misshapen gargoyle expression and its mother was staring straight at me.

I had to keep the same look on my face and divert my gaze to something else, so she wouldn't suspect. I flicked through some crayon-scarred Beano annuals with a look of apparent disgust. A minute later she was still staring. We left.

• • •

Slowly, ever so slowly, we've started to get into a routine. Certain members of the family have suggested that this is more by luck than judgement – Oliver certainly does seem to have settled naturally into a good pattern of behaviour. But I'd like to think there's a bit of nurture in there as well.

Sorting out the feeding was a big factor. Elle expresses all Oliver's feeds and we try to stay one in front at all times. He's on to the bottle now – the cup feeding was messy and inefficient and I don't think Elle's nerves could stand feeding him directly from the breast. This way round, we know how much he's drinking and he still gets the right nutrients.

He feeds every four hours, almost like clockwork, so in the

evenings he has milk at 9pm, goes to bed, we collapse on the sofa then follow him up to bed an hour or so later, he wakes at 1am, we get up and feed him, then it's the same again at 5am and 9am.

We're both getting at least our basic four hours' sleep a night. A few weeks ago, four hours' sleep would have left me as a grouchy zombie. Today, it's blissful.

Other parts of life fit in around this regime. We get up, get dressed, go for walks – I've even started to work again. The health visitor has continued the midwives' vague attitude to appointment times, so we've ended up missing her on a few occasions – she's as skilful at the rude notes as the midwife. We're mobile, we're calm and we've got a plan. In short, I guess we're getting confident.

Chapter Five
The first three months

"Two key tips: be organised, as it helps preserve your sanity; and use every bit of outside help available." R, dad of one.

What's happening?

One to three months

Your baby – As your baby's senses develop, the outside world will become much more interesting. Sights, sounds and smells are all absorbing and your baby's responsiveness is the first sign of a developing personality. Your baby's motor skills (hand-eye co-ordination rather than handbrake turns) are improving and this is reflected in their ability to make a grab for anything and everything that passes close by – dad's fingers, dogs' tails, other babies etc.

Your partner – At six weeks your partner will be asked to visit her GP or the hospital for a check up to make sure everything is OK. This is as much a check of her emotional state as her physical well-being, but principally, if your partner's had surgery during the birth the doctor will check that any wounds are healing well and she will also run checks on urine, blood pressure and weight to check everything is normal.

Confidence gets your chin up, but only so that you won't see the banana skin on the pavement. This morning Elle had a lie-in. I fed the boy without drama, then he and I gazed at the cricket scorecards on text. All was calm. Then Oliver's face went red and a rumble came from his nappy region.

I sighed, collected the nappy changing stuff with the coolness of a pro and laid him down. The clumsy uncertainty of that first change was a distant, laughable memory.

I cleaned him up and was reaching for the fresh nappy when his sprinkler system went off and sprayed liberal amounts of wee around the room. I was reaching for the cotton wool when his bowels erupted, showering the remainder of the room and my legs in stinking crap. I was reaching for a towel when he burped, sending a whoosh of stinky milk from his mouth. Then suddenly there was more of the sticky greenish-brown slime from his bum. So much poo. "Help," I screamed. "Help me."

Elle sprinted down the stairs, and quickly arrived at a scene of chaos. Oliver was floating happily in a congealing mixture of bodily fluids and I was shaking my head and mopping furiously. "It's coming out of everywhere," I sobbed. "It just won't stop."

Fortunately the relief that I hadn't broken her son calmed the fury she must have felt at being scared half to death by my bloodcurdling scream. She elbowed me out of the way and got things sorted. Oliver's not yet smiled at me, but I swear he's frowned a dozen times. I'm fairly sure I heard him tut once.

This nappy from hell is a warning that I shouldn't start getting overconfident. It's a valuable lesson and one that will carry me through the next week or so of health visitor and doctor checks before the fateful day that sees us released into the world as fully functioning, independent parents.

• • •

We've not seen our GP since Elle was about 20 weeks pregnant. So much seems to have changed in that time it was refreshing to speak to someone who had no opinion on the manner of Oliver's upbringing. All she cared about in this six week check was whether he was progressing as expected (he was) and whether Elle was getting back to good health (she was). It was a welcome, highlight free confirmation of progress. After poking, prodding and weighing Oliver, she left him naked on the change mat. Before I could say 'you don't want to do that' he'd pissed all over a wide range of medical supplies.

The GP also checked Elle's caesarean scar to make sure it was healed, and asked a load of personal questions about exercise and getting back to pre-pregnancy weight, which she's doing steadily. I hadn't really given that much thought to Elle's physical appearance. There hasn't been time or inclination. Sleep is still the prime concern.

What are you looking at?

Your partner's body

You may be a bit shocked by how slowly your partner's pre-pregnancy figure is returning, but you know in your heart that criticising her on the subject would mean certain death (or at least a night sleeping in the shed). A better alternative would be to help your partner regain her slender shape by encouraging her in two key ways:

Food. The food your partner eats is still being converted into essential nutrients for the baby, through her breast milk. So she will need to eat well for the next few months. However, eating a lot of empty calories won't help her or the baby. She needs to cut out fatty foods and eat plenty of starchy vegetables as well as salad, fruit, eggs and fish. If you want her to look her best, you could offer to cook more and gradually introduce high energy, low calorie food into your diet.

Exercise. The best way to eliminate the post-baby bulge is to keep going on the pelvic floor exercises that were recommended during late pregnancy. In addition, some abdominal exercises should help. Three or four times a day your partner should lie on her back, with her back flat on the floor, then curl her head and shoulder off the floor towards her knees. Going up slowly (say for a count of ten) and then back slowly (x20) will help her tone her tummy in no time. You could do them too and get shot of the beer belly.

Aside of the exercises, you can also encourage her to go for some medium-length walks with the baby. Walking and swimming are about the best forms of exercise post-birth and they can be done easily with junior in tow.

After poking, prodding and weighing Oliver, she left him naked on the change mat. Before I could say 'you don't want to do that' he'd pissed all over a wide range of medical supplies. All in all, an excellent appointment.

The health visitor's sign-off was an altogether stranger experience. Elle was asked a series of simple questions on a sliding points scale, rather like those 'are you a great lover?' tests in glossy magazines. But the subject of this test was a bit more mundane, bleak even. 'Have you contemplated hurting your baby?' – score one point. 'Have you actually hurt your baby?' – score zero points.

At first glance, the idea of the sign-off test appears to be catching out all the suicidal, manically depressed mothers who have up to that point put on a brave face but who just can't resist surveys. It's more likely this is an acknowledgment by the health visitors that they don't have enough time to notice things going seriously wrong.

A new low

Coping with depression

Post-natal depression (PND) is a very broad complaint. It ranges from feelings like isolation and severe tiredness right through to full scale depression. The range of treatments is equally broad – from hormone balancing drugs to counselling and support groups. Symptoms can start to show soon after birth or much later – the most common include exhaustion, tearfulness, disorientation and lack of self-esteem.

What about you? Do you recognise any of these symptoms in yourself? Male post-natal depression is now recognised as a serious issue – for the first time clinics are beginning to offer dedicated support for men. Most male PND sufferers become affected because their partner is suffering, but that's not always the case.

So if you or your partner find yourselves suffering from these symptoms, contact your doctor or speak to the health visitor and get some treatment. It's not a sign of your weakness or inability to cope – but failing to acknowledge the symptoms could lead to serious problems.

Fortunately Elle passed, or at least we think she did. The scoring system was a bit complicated, and given that the previous test I took claimed I wasn't a great lover, I've lost faith in the accuracy of such things. Most importantly it was enough to convince the health visitor that we weren't 'at risk'. With a clean bill of mental and physical health, we have graduated as parents after six weeks of thankless hard work. Everything else should be a stroll in the park.

After six long weeks confined to base we are really going places – Oliver's first holiday is to be a UK tour on an epic scale. First stop is my parents' house on the south coast then home for a few days, then on up north to see Elle's sister.

This trip has been planned on a military scale – Elle has written long lists of items to take – our dining table has been taken over as a store for the various odds and ends that Oliver will need over the long weekend.

My role as defined in 'the list' is roadie and driver, which is a bit better than Elle's task of keeping a baby and two dogs happy for four hours.

"Did we pack the baby?"

Managing trips away

Welcome back to normality – or at least to something that comes pretty close. The first proper trip away feels like a milestone, whether it comes days, weeks or months after your baby's arrival in the world.

Unfortunately it can also be a millstone – your carefully organised routine goes out of the window as you struggle to fit into other households. This struggle is partly logistical – on our first trip away baby stuff took up about 80 per cent of the available space, 15 per cent was dog stuff, leaving just 5 per cent for a shared toothbrush and a change of underwear (briefs, of course). Almost all of the nappy stuff we packed for Oliver could have been bought at our destination and we overestimated wildly on clothes and toys, but we tried to plan for all situations.

The level of preparation required for a short trip away is actually minimal – make sure you've got the means to feed, change and clothe the baby and that there's somewhere suitable for the baby to sleep at the other end. Everything else can be managed as and when.

The harder part of getting away is coping with a different regime when your own life is so clearly fixed around the baby. It can feel quite rude to be forever asking your hosts to turn down the heating, draw the curtains, turn off the TV or whisper in their own house – yet these may be essential parts of your home routine.

You can also feel pretty stressed about the noise coming from your baby at three in the morning while everyone struggles to sleep. Get your hosts to bend on things that really matter to you – safety issues like temperature – and learn to adapt to those that won't or can't be changed.

Travel is supposed to broaden the mind, and while our travels haven't always been a huge success, they have slowly introduced our son to a world outside of his immediate routine – and that can only be good for the future.

Packing the car was a bit of a challenge. Lesser men would have given up, but I didn't spend my college years playing 'Tetris' for nothing. It all went in, though I don't have a clue if it'll ever come out again, or if any of it will work when it does.

We had a few flashpoints over certain items, all of which I ended up conceding, but the one item that simply wouldn't squeeze in is probably the most important of all – the swing.

Ah, the swing. The greatest invention known to man. The friends who recommended it assured us that we'd come to adore it, but when Oliver rejected it on that first night I thought we'd wasted our money. How wrong I was. So many times in the last few weeks we've longed with every bone in our bodies for Oliver to nap, and the swing has done the trick. It's magical and beautiful and I even forgive the ghastly plinky-plonky music it spews out. But it's huge and it must stay at home. I miss it already.

The journey wasn't bad, especially as Oliver slept through most of it. The worst part was my driving. I've become so negative and defensive behind the wheel, honking and gesturing like an Italian in a hurry. I'm aware of this strange habit, but there doesn't seem to be anything I can do about it. My car, my road, my rules.

Somehow, in spite of this, we made it, unpacked the car before nightfall and relaxed into our first night away as a family. Oliver took a while to go off in the strange surroundings, but now he's settled, and we've a great dinner and a good laugh, our first proper meal in company since the birth. It feels good to be away.

• • •

What a night. Easily the worst since that first night at home. Oliver slept until about midnight, then woke wanting a feed and wouldn't settle again. He was really angry, very noisy and I was acutely aware that we'd have the whole house awake if he kept going. Elle was exhausted so she went back off to bed and I tried to keep Oliver quiet. I went through my whole routine, rocking him and singing to him.

As the hours ticked by I changed him, fed him again and wandered around my parents' house, desperate to keep him calm. I thought about taking him out in the car, but it's never a foolproof answer. I needed the swing. I knew I needed it, and I suspect he did too. No amount of waggling him around could imitate the experience. When my mum came into the lounge at about 7am, I was dead on my feet. She took him and I crawled back off to bed where Elle and I both slept until midday.

My parents spent the morning walking Oliver around the garden in his pram, gently coaxing him to sleep. He got a couple of hours but not enough to improve his mood. A sleepless night hasn't done much for us either – we're both a bit snappy, which makes us particularly unpleasant house guests.

My dad's keeping out of the way – I don't think babies are his thing. In fact he admitted last night that when I was born he took up doing the washing and ironing just to avoid getting roped into baby care.

He has a point. Much though I love my son, I'd be very happy to avoid the less appealing elements of his care – like nappies and midnight battles. It's hard to find nannies who just do the nightshift and are happy to be paid minimum wage, so the chances are we're going to have to carry on sharing the burden between us.

While I moan about it, it's better than the alternative – I think my dad probably regrets not spending more time with his children as babies, but I'm sure he didn't feel there was much alternative at the time. Now that there is an alternative, I'm not going to shirk my responsibilities for the sake of a decent kip.

Chores of disapproval

Establishing a routine at home

Speaking of responsibilities and routines, the wider horizon of a trip away gives you the perfect chance to reflect on the division of labour in the home.

It's reasonable to expect your partner to be focused chiefly on the baby up to this point, but if that leaves you with a large burden of washing, cooking and cleaning you're not likely to want to come home at the end of a working day.

If you can afford to employ someone to help with the chores, that's great – if you can bribe a family member to do it for free, that's even better. Some things can be farmed out much more easily than others – look in local services directories for ironing services, or for a cleaner who will come in an do a couple of hours a week just to keep on top of the mess.

The important thing is that you spend as much of your time at home actually building a relationship with your child, not with your washing machine. Plan a rota of domestic duties and make sure everyone sticks to it – this might seem a bit too organised, but at least it creates an air of industry and protects your valuable quality time with the baby.

Given that we're barely conscious, my mum probably could have offered to take Oliver off our hands for the rest of the day, but I'm glad she hasn't. Our families are forced to walk a fine line between being supportive and muscling in. My parents err on the side of caution, but I hope that's because they are confident we'll cope with the journey to successful parenthood ourselves. It would be an easier ride if they did it all for us, but it would take one hell of a lot longer to get there.

All this deep though is due to the fact that I can't understand why our son is so miserable. At home he's become a dream, a really easy baby. Everyone grinds their teeth with envy when we tell them about peaceful family trips to the pub or single feed nights where we all get eight hours sleep. But as soon as we come away it all appears to mean nothing.

I can't work out whether he's upset because we've broken the routine, or whether he's picking up our anxiety at being away from home for the first time. I had no idea I'd find it this stressful – halfway through the first leg of our tour and I've completely lost the taste for travel.

• • •

I'd like to say it got better, but actually it didn't. I just got more practiced at coping without sleep and dealing with a frustrated and grouchy baby. While Oliver slept a little better at Elle's sister's house, we had worse nights, lying awake and expecting the worst.

The main problem is the contrast between these visits and their pre-baby versions. Both destinations have been places we've gone to have a few drinks, enjoy good food and relax. Now we are left in no doubt as to the purpose of the visit – our hosts rush over to Oliver, pick him up and coo lovingly at him while we struggle in with the bags, cot and accessories. We've even had to make our own cups of tea. To be fair, we're not the same people any more either – I've become incredibly tense, worrying that Oliver will disturb lovingly prepared meals, or keep our hosts awake all night.

It's not his fault, he didn't ask to be dragged around the country visiting people, but if we can't find a way to manage it without sleep deprivation and stress then we'll have to stay at home for the foreseeable future. The experience has made me realise just how fragile our home 'routine' actually is – we've created an artificial situation that makes him comfortable and makes our lives easier, but it has no relation to real life. We've become prisoners of our own routine and if a couple of weekends away can trip us up so badly, I can't imagine how we're going to maintain this uneasy status quo.

On a brighter note, we're just a couple of weeks away from our first Christmas as a family, and we've decided to stay at home. It's not a very popular choice among the wider family, but given our dreadful travels, we don't see any alternative. Anyway, I want to be selfish this year, Oliver may not remember his first Christmas, but I will and I don't want other people spoiling my/his big day.

· · ·

This is a tale of two needles. Yesterday we went out and bought our Christmas tree. It's ridiculously early to be buying it, but I'm so excited about Christmas I couldn't help myself.

We rigged Oliver up in his baby carrier and strapped him to Elle's front, facing the world. And he loved it. I know I'm frequently guilty of filling in an awful lot of blanks in his personality, but something about the trip clearly had him engrossed. Maybe the street decorations and lights helped, but it was the first time I've seen him acknowledge strangers – and he was definitely smiling. At one stage he even whistled 'Silent Night'.

Our tree is modest and guaranteed zero needle drop,

which probably means it's already long dead. Oliver stared at it with a mixture of wonder and suspicion as it jogged along on the seat next to him on the drive home.

Hello cool world

Interaction with your baby

From around six weeks onwards, your baby's interaction with the world starts to increase – you might even get your first smile.

When Oliver started to interact, I was like a kid with a new bike on Christmas day, I wanted to get out and about and start playing with him. But while babies are more fun round about now, there are only a limited number of things they can do – and they can easily be over-stimulated by the antics of an excited dad.

This is especially true if you have a boy and want to encourage rough-and-tumble from an early age. Elle's dad was particularly keen to whirl Oliver around as much as possible, and while it probably wasn't doing any harm, it was agony to watch as an overprotective parent – and probably wasn't a barrel of laughs for the little chap either.

In the first couple of months, gentle play is better for the baby – musical games and toys with a range of textures to hold are great for stimulation.

If yesterday was his favourite trip out, today was most likely his worst – a short journey to the doctor for his first round of inoculations. In principle, baby jabs are an excellent idea. In practice they are an excellent way to give babies an early and important lesson in fearing the medical profession.

A jab in the dark?

Immunising your baby

Immunisation is a subject that's guaranteed to split opinion. Everyone sees the logic in it, but no-one can be absolutely certain it isn't harming babies in other ways.

The biggest bone of contention is MMR (Measles, Mumps and Rubella) the jab that your child is given around 12-15 months. Some research suggests a link to autism, but that goes against government opinion.

It's a subject that you can research in detail, but in a nutshell your child is only safe if immunised. How you choose to have the drugs administered is a matter of patient choice – but opting out altogether is a terrible idea, dangerous for your baby, and for all other children.

Few parents raise objections to the first round of immunisations – given at two to four months. These are for hib (a type of flu), diphtheria, tetanus, meningitis C and whooping cough. It's normally a two stage process and may carry mild side effects like a slightly raised temperature and swelling around the needle mark.

The doctors' surgery was clearly having a mass jab fest, as the waiting room was packed with nervous mums and dads and edgy babies. None of us spoke, we all focused our attention on our offspring, making sure they were calm and relaxed. A voice would crackle over the PA, calling families into a side room. The waiting masses kept their focus and talked in stage whispers. Then a cry would ring out and suddenly the noise level would rise like an angry bee swarm to mask the screams.

The parents would come out, clutching their sobbing child, heads down, and were sent on a detour of the waiting room to avoid upsetting the unsuspecting babies. Another name was called and the process started over.

When it came to our turn, Oliver gazed with innocent curiosity at the long suffering and tired looking nurse. She kept the needle out of his sight and it seemed to take him by surprise. For a minute it appeared he wouldn't even flinch. But then his face crumbled and his skin reddened and he bellowed. It was just the one cry, he was sniffling as we took him back to the car, but I felt like we'd been willing participants in his introduction to the cruel world.

The nurse warned us that there might be some side effects, but he slept when we got home and we figured he'd had no reaction at all. But then he woke up and screamed. He screamed until he was purple in the face and wouldn't be consoled or distracted or amused. He was a picture of misery and for the first time as a parent I convinced myself that he was seriously ill.

I wanted to drive him straight to hospital but Elle wanted to take a look in the baby books first. All they did was repeat the nurse's comments. By the time we'd finished faffing around and arguing over treatments he'd given up yelling and had gone back to sleep.

Elle went out to do some Christmas shopping and I sat and watched him fretfully, watching his breathing and holding my hands close to his face just in case heat was radiating from him. It's a miracle he didn't wake up again.

It's really shaken me up. He was only upset for about 20 minutes, but it was such a long and heartfelt display of misery that I was convinced something dreadful would happen. And I was hopeless in the face of that. Worse than hopeless – I wanted to take him straight to the hospital like all the jumpy, paranoid parents I used to laugh at.

Why wasn't I calm and in control? Why did I have to make the situation 10 times worse with my own worries?

He woke as Elle returned, and while he's been a bit woozy, there's been no repeat of the screaming fit. Next time I swear I'll know what to do.

Sick with worry

Common baby illnesses

Dealing with illness is a pretty demanding task at the best of times, but when the midwives and health visitors have retreated into the background and you are left with a baby and a range of potentially life-threatening illnesses your mind does start to play tricks. To give you a better idea of what to look for, here's a guide to some of the more serious signs of illness in a baby. You should contact a doctor/the hospital immediately if your baby experiences any of the following difficulties:

Breathing. Call the doctor if you baby has difficulty breathing, or makes pronounced grunting or wheezing sounds while breathing, orif the breath becomes irregular or if your baby's skin turns blue or pale.

Fits and drowsiness. If your baby makes sudden jerky movements or if they are very hard to wake up or seem totally disorientated, seek medical help.

Rashes. Lots of babies get rashes, especially early on, but a rash of red spots may be a sign of a potentially serious blood infection. Press a glass to the rash. If the red spots disappear under the pressure of the glass all is OK, but if the spots remain, get help straight away.

Feeding problems. If your baby unusually refuses feeds, you should seek medical help, likewise if your baby is repeatedly sick (especially in conjunction with diarrhoea) there is a danger of dehydration and this can lead to serious problems.

In general. While you don't want to be rushing to casualty at the first sign of anything remotely out of the ordinary, it doesn't always pay to wait and see. If your baby is behaving in an unusual manner or seems totally out of sorts, hot, cold or listless, call the doctor, or at least given NHS Direct a ring.

•   •   •

Two months and a few days after Oliver was born we've

had our first night out. Elle's dad was the babysitter and the occasion was pre-Christmas drinks and a meal with Elle's work colleagues.

We'd been to a few of these work socials pre-baby, and as a general rule I filled the role of little wife, chatting with the spouses while Elle and her colleagues enjoyed their break from work by talking about…work. Now Elle is a mother she has a link to the spouses, and I have the sympathy of the men. I'm not sure either of us is comfortable in these new roles.

Saturday night's alright (for sleeping)

Your shrinking social life

Back when I was childless and fancy-free, I used to taunt friends who were parents with tales of crazy exploits like trips to the cinema, restaurants and pubs. Their jaws would slacken as I told them I'd stopped out until after 11pm or stayed in bed until lunchtime. It was great fun, and I never tired of it.

The simple truth is one or both of you will lose a big part of your social life for some time – and while some people aren't at all bothered by this, others act like they've lost a limb. It doesn't matter which type you are, you need to get out and party again, if not within weeks of the birth, then within a couple of months.

Going out alone. Spending time with your mates, even the childless ones (shock, horror) is a good way of stepping outside of the routine of baby care. If they are good mates they will even listen patiently while you spend the first half hour slagging off your partner, the health visitor, the NHS or whoever is feeling the force of your fury at that point in time. After that, you can settle into the evening proper, but you do need the ranting time, it's like shedding a skin and without that your frustration could well boil over into something more serious.

Going out together. Time out of the house is important to your sanity and your stress levels, but more than anything else, it's important to your relationship with your partner. She may not be too happy about leaving the baby, she may even actively dislike the idea, but she needs to take it on trust that getting out is good for rediscovering why you're together in the first place. Don't be tempted to put it off, the longer you leave it, the harder it will be to trust someone else to look after your child.

Sit...stay. A good babysitter is a friend for life, a bad babysitter may well set your social life back years, so choose your babysitter carefully – adult friends or family members are good, if a little inclined to experiment with their own unique baby care methods, teenage girls with Hell's Angel boyfriends are bad – somewhere between the two is a happy medium. You'll find a good list of recommended names at the clinic, or at the local college (especially if they run childcare courses). When you do leave junior with someone new for the first time, be sure you've made a sound choice – to the extent of actually interviewing the prospective candidates – and leave a comprehensive (though not novel-length) list of dos and don'ts for the sitter to follow. This should include details of routines, allergies, any medication that's OK for the baby and naturally any emergency contact numbers.

Elle had to work especially hard at the party as her firm has a new managing director who has never even met her. However much her colleagues might have built her up, his view will be coloured by the fact he's currently paying her not to work. Listening to the blokes around tonight, you'd assume she's on some fantastic stress free holiday.

I know Elle misses work and I know she's frustrated at not being up to speed with the changes in the company. It's contrived to make her feel like even more of an outsider. But she is, and so am I – despite my hearty laughter at the cynical jokes about women's work – because a major part of us is at home. We've changed, we've become more detached from the outside world, and perhaps less vulnerable to its criticisms and pressures.

In the past I've watched this in other new parents and I've mistaken it for vanity or selfishness. At its worst it's self-absorption, at its best it's a kind of force field, a mutual strength of purpose.

We were the first to leave.

•   •   •

And so to Christmas. Elle and I have vastly different ideas of what constitutes a family Christmas. For her, it's a huge social gathering of the greater family, a chance to catch up with the uncles, aunts and cousins that you haven't seen for a year. For me it's immediate family only, lots of food, drink and presents – especially presents. We've had a good go at sampling each other's ideal Christmases over the years, but this year my model won hands down.

I haven't been this excited about Christmas for ages, and I can't really explain why I'm so upbeat about it now. I've been pestering Elle for days to let me open some presents early, but she patiently told me to wait.

Because there's a child in the house I have this sense that Christmas should be magical again. So all the old weepy movies have come out, carols are being played on the stereo for the first time in years, the hall is decked with boughs of holly and the door has a giant wreath. Oliver is unmoved, though he likes the carols – they seem to work just like lullabies.

On the big day everything went to plan – the food, drink and presents were fantastic. Oliver – tired from watching me open all his presents – slept quietly in his carrycot throughout lunch and woke just as I was sitting down with my port in front of the afternoon movie. It was blissful, if slightly unreal.

I'm already aware that it's the calm before the storm – and I don't just mean the upcoming family visits. From January onwards, life takes on a much more serious edge.

Chapter Six
The first six months

"I seriously recommend having a pot of gold available as a fall back – having money to get through the hard times eases the pressure." L, dad of three.

What's happening?

Three to six months

Your baby – Playing with your baby will be a much more interactive experience by now, and all the money you saved when you resisted buying the redundant 0-3 month toys can now be splurged on fancy goods like baby gyms and balls. Your baby will love rolling around on the floor and may even have started to master the art of rolling right over and holding their head up in a sort-of 'crawling sniper' position. This is the first step towards first steps, as the baby that gets mobile can see the tangible benefits of travelling from one place to another and may, consequently, be ready to experiment with crawling or bottom shuffling. A six-month-old baby should be able to sit up with minimal support, which will be a real asset when it comes to getting into the high chair for feeding time.

Your partner – Depending on the kind of maternity leave your partner is entitled to, she may well be thinking about heading back to work in some capacity during this period. As well as the practical considerations of weaning the baby off breast milk and organising childcare, there's a strong chance that your partner will experience a strong emotional wrench at the prospect of being separated from the baby. Granted, she may be delighted by the prospect of spending time with some actual grown-ups, but a deep, everlasting bond has developed between mother and child that you need to keep in mind if her mood is affected around the time of the return to work.

First day of the new year and I'm in a seriously bad mood. The parents-in-law came over yesterday and offered to look after Oliver while Elle and I went out to the cinema. When we got back, he was wrapped in about 16 layers of clothing and was moody and tired.

They love him very much, and I'm really happy for them

to spend time with him, but they are obsessed with keeping him warm and awake. Since he missed his nap he was miserable and hard work all evening, and I wasn't doing a very good job of concealing my irritation that our careful instructions had been so wilfully ignored.

We got to midnight, toasted the New Year and went to bed – except Elle and I were up several times in the night with Oliver. So I spent this morning sulking until Elle's parents left and now I'm hiding at my desk, trying to find the motivation to start the new year in positive fashion.

I've got to do something about this moodiness. I might feel as if I'm being a good father to Oliver, but I'm not being a good father to the outside world. I'm too quick to criticise people who try to help, and to condemn people who don't.

Part of my brain realises that Elle's parents are doing what comes naturally – they're attempting to care for their grandchild using methods that worked for them as new parents, which is perfectly reasonable. But that part of my brain is controlled by sleep levels – too little sleep and I begin to wonder how they could possibly dare to come into my house and not follow my instructions to the letter.

Like my hangover, the regret I feel at being so offhand with the family is taking a while to clear. They would have to do something massively stupid to actually harm Oliver, and that's not going to happen, so it's time I cut them a bit of slack.

This year's resolution is to chill out as a dad, stop getting wound up over things I can't control and learn to handle the family. That should keep me occupied for a while.

• • •

Finding things to occupy me shouldn't be a problem. What I need to find is time. Elle's been into the office and has worked out a schedule for returning to work that involves going back part time from the beginning of February. She's starting off at just two days a week, moving to three in March and then to four from April onwards. That's more work days than we'd originally planned, but it's as much of a concession as she could squeeze out of her boss.

So in a matter of weeks life is going to change big time.

I'm going to go from a supporting role to part time carer, then eventually to full time with Oliver. I'll be writing in the gaps around my other duties, which is something I'm used to. But I haven't a clue how this is going to work.

Day care daddy?

Your childcare choices

It's increasingly common for babies to go into nursery from around three to six months and stay there until pre-school. This gives both parents a shot at continuing their careers and ensures neither feels left behind professionally. It's not a cheap option – depending on the amount of childcare required and the area you live in, you may find yourself paying anything from £300-£500 per week.

This isn't what we chose to do – but I'm not going to stand in judgement of it, there's no right and wrong way to juggle the work/childcare balance, only the way that suits your situation. With both parents at work, there's a significant cut in financial stress – if one person loses their job, it isn't the end of the world. But that doesn't mean it's the only option.

A growing number of men would like to stay at home with their children and this is an important trend. It's not an easy option – it's much more of a vocation than a vacation – but there is absolutely nothing stopping you from being an ideal main carer, particularly if you approach this time with the energy, drive and commitment you'd give to any new job.

If you're both lucky enough to work in one of the few trades that encourages and supports flexible working, it is definitely worth considering this option. Under recent government legislation, your employer is obliged to consider your request for flexible working and either agree or provide you with a business case of why it isn't possible. With a bit of haggling, you may be able to organise a day of work from home or a shorter working week. Check out the DTI website (**www.dti.gov.uk**) for more information on flexible working for parents.

Our ideal scenario was each to work a three day week, take on childcare duties for the other three, and have one family day together. We're still working on it, but when we get there it'll be good news for everyone.

Meanwhile, we've had more jabs to deal with. This time we bought some baby medicine as a preventive and gave it to Oliver after the shock and pain of the needle prick had died down. It did the trick, no nasty reaction or afternoon tantrum.

But the damage was done after the first jab, when he developed a taste for the full-on yell if provoked. He uses it sparingly, but it can cut through metre-thick walls. It certainly derails my train of thought while I'm trying to work in my makeshift study in the bedroom.

I've developed my plan to make a sneaky return to the room formerly known as the 'study' – currently Oliver's nursery – and expand my empire once more. It's not just that my workspace feels temporary, my whole working life feels temporary. With the prospect of spending the majority of the week as Oliver's sole carer, I'm seriously wondering if I'll be able to manage any work beyond fatherhood. Reclaiming the study would at least be a statement of intent, even if it wasn't then followed up with any actual work.

I put the idea to Elle, and she seemed OK with it on the condition that she got a decent wardrobe in the bedroom in place of my desk and that I had to do all the heavy lifting. It's a deal worth making – I'm going back in. I'll have to share the room with a bed full of soft toys and a suspicious pile of crocheted jackets, but these are small matters in my struggle to retain at least some small sense of self.

Some people might think I'm overplaying my push for independence – especially as I'm yet to spend a full day alone with Oliver. But the rules of battle are drawn, and he knows where I stand. Bring it on.

• • •

Last night I had a terrible dream. Alien invaders had spotted humanity's key weakness – an inability to resist the charm of cute babies. They'd parachuted millions of sweet, angelic little bundles to Earth where they were immediately adopted by happy, loving parents. But they turned out to be devastating time bombs and by the time we found out, it was too late.

No need to wake Sigmund Freud from the dead to discover the meaning behind that one. I'm scared of being responsible for Oliver – scared of what might go wrong if we're left alone together for any length of time.

I'm going to try and deal with this irrational fear by facing it head on. Elle's going to be spending odd days at work before going back in earnest, so I have plenty of chances to spend short periods alone with Oliver before I have to look after him regularly.

At the end of this month I will come head to head with another of my ongoing nightmares – dealing with the family – as we're planning an incredible 300 mile round trip to visit Elle's parents, my parents and then head off on holiday in Wales, where we'll be joined by Elle's parents (again), sister and brother-in-law. We don't believe in half measures.

• • •

This is a strange period of readjustment. Since I moved back into the study I've been really possessive over my working time, and really moody when I'm disturbed by noise from downstairs. That's pretty hard on Elle, who can only do so much to keep the boy quiet.

She's begun the slow and difficult process of removing herself from him. We're working out ways to wean him gradually off breast milk – Elle's never going to be able to work in her ultra-male office environment and still express milk every day.

She's actually only had one day back in the office this month – and that wasn't even a full day. It gave me long enough to head out in the car with Oliver for the first time.

After about five minutes I realised I hadn't bought a bag with nappies or any of the million accessories that are normally crammed into Elle's pockets, bag and shoes before any normal journey gets underway. But this was no normal journey – this was a badly prepared journey. I crossed my fingers and put my foot down.

As Oliver has shown few signs of likes and dislikes, I had to take a few liberties with the choice of venue for this first trip. We could have sat in the park, but it was hardly the weather. We could have gone to the zoo, but he might have been frightened by the animals. Much better to take him to a quiet, calm, dry and warm bookshop, where I could, by coincidence, spend a happy hour browsing for books.

His mother must have had a word with him before we set out, because he took against the bookshop almost immediately, shattering the 'no talking above a whisper' rule with a series of ear-splitting shrieks. He appeared to be hell-bent on testing his alarm, so after just 10 minutes I made some rash purchases, then wondered dumbly what to do with him for the rest of the day.

We drove to a lake, where Oliver watched me as I watched

the wading birds and ate an ice cream. This isn't a common event in January, but it wasted another five minutes. Then we took the long way home. Total journey time – around two and a half hours. Total journey cost – around £25. I have to get better at planning days out.

The young and the restless

Managing time alone with the baby

It should be so easy to take care of a baby. They are small, full of wonder at the world around them and they make few financial demands. And yet I still contrived to make the experience stressful and full of difficulties.

Be prepared. The first rule of spending time alone with your baby is to understand the baby's routine – naps, feeds, etc. – and stick to it, even if that spoils your fantastic day long trip to a baby theme park. Don't be too ambitious and don't forget to pack all the essentials you'll need for even the shortest trip – nappies, bags, wipes and a change of clothes.

Some of my friends, with the best intentions, try to make their time with the baby extra special by going go-karting or abseiling or something equally dumb. This time is not a test of how cool or responsible you are as a dad – that'll come much later in your child's development and the baby won't be impressed by your efforts.

The best bet now is to spend as much time as possible interacting with your baby, whether that means taking them for a walk or just sitting on a rug in the garden, it's about creating a simple, stress free environment.

Safety first. If you're together for a whole day, or even a weekend, it's important to have somewhere safe for the baby to play while you're briefly out of the room. Stern baby manuals will tell you never to leave the baby alone, but they don't tell you never to answer the door, telephone or call of nature. A decent, secure playpen is a must – you can get ones that fold down to almost nothing. Beyond that it's simply a case of making it up as you go along. Don't panic if there's some friction – you can't reason with a baby, so there's no point trying to argue the toss, but they're predictable and easily distracted, so if yours is grizzling then change the subject and keep changing it until you find something that works.

Just in case things take a turn for the worst, make sure you know where the medicines are stored and where your baby's healthcare record book is kept.

Quality time – playing with your responsive child. Play and free time with your child is reaching that critical phase where you're starting to have real influence. This can be good or bad depending on whether your influence is active (playing games, engaging whenever possible) or passive (just performing menial tasks at the start and end of the day).

No-one pretends the work/life juggle is an easy trick, but it's possible to make the most of a bad situation by really improving the time you do have together. From about four months onwards babies are real sponges for information, so activities like reading, singing and playing simple 'peek-a-boo' games have huge rewards.

If you can 'own' a particular part of your baby's routine – bath time or bed time are good starting points – then you can focus on making them as fun and interactive as possible. The more reaction you get, the more satisfying the experience becomes.

Life seems to be a process of setting new roles and responsibilities, with Elle and me both keen to keep as much time back for ourselves as possible. While the last three months haven't been too hard – certainly not as hard as the three months running up to the birth – it hasn't been all champagne and flowers either.

Apart from the odd night out, we've had very little time together as a couple and sex has naturally slipped down the agenda a bit – especially as Oliver continues to share our bedroom. Part of the reason behind our holiday in Wales is to let the family look after Oliver while we spend quality time together before the new working arrangement kicks in.

· · ·

It all started so well. Oliver coped brilliantly with a really long day in the car and only started moaning on the Severn Bridge. I was doing about 50mph and the wind and rain were lashing the car, but I could still draw from the deep well of optimism that goes with the start of a holiday.

Though it took another two hours of driving through darkness and storms before we found the cottage, it was still worth it. The place was fantastic, Oliver went straight to sleep, we celebrated with a bottle of wine and went to bed full of excitement for the coming days.

It got even better in the morning, we used the swimming pool and wandered in the garden. It was heaven. We were more relaxed than we've been for weeks, months even.

Elle's parents arrived – but still things were great. They loved the cottage, we all sat by the pool, Oliver even had a quick dip. By the time Elle's sister arrived things had started to get a bit tense. My 'no shouting at the in-laws' resolution wasn't holding, and our very particular way of bringing up our son was clashing with the parents-in-law's equally deep held beliefs. They kept pushing him to do new things, to roll over, to play with the toys they'd brought for him – I'd rather just let him find his own way. Elle would rather avoid a fight.

We decided to get some space, and went into the nearby town for a wander. She urged me to be calm, just for a couple more days.

When we got back, everyone was in the sauna. No, my mistake, they were in the living room. It was as hot as a sauna. Oliver, woken from his torpor by our arrival, screamed his head off until I took him into a cooler room.

I looked like an idiot, huffing and puffing and generally communicating my anger in as many non-verbal ways as I could manage. The trouble is, I'm the one who looks like he's throwing his dummy out of the pram, as if I'm the overprotective parent who believes it's bad news that his son's been boiled alive in someone else's care. Well, maybe I am overreacting, but that's not a crime and the least I deserve is some understanding from those around me.

Like all new fathers I feel a big responsibility to my child, but I feel it even more seriously as I'm soon to be solely responsible for his welfare for large parts of the day. I have to prove to myself and others that I'm competent, but if I keep reacting so strongly to their attitudes and well meaning mistakes, I'm never going to manage it.

I'm stretching the desire to be a good father to the point of obsession, and there's no room in my plan for 'live and let live' – when I come up against similarly stubborn beliefs, all I can do is clash with them. That's not fair on Elle and it's not even fair on the family. Must try harder.

• • •

A couple of weeks into the new routine and I'm happy with life. OK, so we haven't hit any bumps yet, but Oliver's napping every morning for at least a couple of hours, which gives me time to work every day. He wakes in time for a lunchtime feed and then the rest of the day is ours – and this is just two days a week. This full time care lark is a doddle.

Even the potential banana skin of weaning seems to have worked out OK. Elle started this on holiday, and I've been carefully following up. Oliver's not a huge fan of the mush I've presented for him to date, but then I find it hard to get excited about pulped fruit and vegetables. We were warned that the downside of weaning is smellier nappies, but so far they've just been more colourful. Pea was a sight to behold.

A solid start

How to help with weaning

Weaning is a subject that's still under debate. Some people think a baby should just be on a milk diet until six months – some argue that it's safe to start introducing some pureed food from around four months. In truth, it has less to do with time and more with your baby's inclinations – if the baby starts to show interest in what you're eating and doesn't seem full after a normal milk feed, then it's probably time to start introducing food.

From **Lad** to **Dad**

The most important thing for fathers to know is that when your child starts weaning, mealtimes are no longer the mother's sole area. Feeding is great one-to-one time, and the novelty of being fed by dad will make the move from milk to solids much more exciting for your baby.

Don't become so involved in the process that you develop a mania for stuffing the poor child with every morsel – from six months until two years your baby's still getting essential nutrition from breast or formula milk (as long as they are drinking around 550-600ml a day), the food part of the diet is mainly about trying new tastes and textures. Your baby will start off with pureed vegetables and fruit, but will quickly be managing a combination of these and some cereals, then on to a more balanced diet of pureed meat and potatoes, until they are basically eating what you eat from around 12-18 months.

Most of all, this time is your chance to be together, so turn the experience into really good bonding time, buy silly spoons and bowls, make silly noises, have fun and don't be tempted to eat it all yourself.

While the weather's still bad I'm not being too adventurous over trips out. I've given him another crack at the bookshop – 15 minutes this time – and we've wandered around our village as well as a couple of nearby towns.

Nothing too stressful, nothing too stimulating. But I have big plans.

Oliver's growing a distinct personality as he gets more mobile. He rolls about on the rug in our lounge and he smiles and gurgles. Little things, but they all make the experience of being in his company more worthwhile. If he was just a static lump I'd get very bored with him very quickly. But we play and I read to him and everything seems to be going in, like he has a real thirst for information. God, listen to me, I sound like the proudest mother on the planet. No, the proudest grandmother.

"If you hold his picture sideways, it's a nuclear reactor."

Competitve Dad Syndrome Stage Three – the boastful dad

If there's one symptom that defines Competitive Dad Syndrome it's pushing your child's achievements. Everyone does it, whether it's via the world's longest and most boastful Christmas round robin or a casually dropped remark about being in the 95th percentile for dribbling.

New dads together are like rutting stags when it comes to the subject of the first tooth and the progress of the crawl. We search for new and even more malicious ways to convince others that our progeny is a prodigy and that theirs is just podgy.

When Oliver was six months old, my dad made him a push-along trolley which he wheeled around the living room while I supported him from behind. Elle took a picture which I later doctored, airbrushing out my hands so that he appeared to be walking unsupported. This was shown to family and friends with a casual air and their expressions of amazement were brushed off with a dismissive wave of the hand. Do I feel cheap for pulling a stunt like that? Never. It's one of the greatest joys of parenthood and I challenge you to trump it.

Don't, however, make the mistake of taking any of it too seriously. All babies reach the same milestones, some are faster than others but all of this is ultimately meaningless – the only thing that counts is that they get there.

In my care he's developed some worrying tastes. He's obsessed with the high interest loan adverts on cable TV. It worries me that there's something in these ads that appeals to a four month old baby, worries me even more that he seems to think we need to consider consolidating our debts into one easy repayment. One of his favourite ads features Carol Vorderman of 'Countdown' fame – and that's another programme that captivates him. This suggests to me that he's very advanced, while other children of his age are just starting to recognise letters and numbers, he's already living like a student.

The idiot box

Watching TV with your baby

There's quite a bit of snobbery about TV – with some 'experts' suggesting children should spend less than one hour a day in front of the box. You can't use the same argument with a baby as they aren't likely to be out kicking a ball instead and they do tend to stay in the same place for long periods regardless.

Television is good for certain senses, programmes with music can be very engaging and the variety of dialects is good for language skills. Visually, programmes that use strong contrasts seem to grab babies' attention – mainly ads and cartoons. I'm not saying it is a key teaching aid for your baby's developing mind, but it's a useful source of entertainment when you need a half hour break and you shouldn't feel guilty about using it that way.

Even though we're getting on fine and having fun, I'm still really relieved when Elle gets home at the end of the day. Looking after a baby of his age all day might not be too physically tiring, but it is involving. If he's awake there's no chance I can wander off to the loo to read the paper for half an hour. He needs me with him all the time, and that's a major commitment.

On the plus side, it's all great bonding time. Elle's started to notice real similarities in personality – we both struggle to get up in the morning and cannot cope until we've had our milk/cup of tea. We both tend to be a bit theatrical when we've got a bump or scratch. We have a mutual love of physical comedy. It's just possible I'm moulding the little chap into my image.

I don't think Elle's jealous of this connection between us. She enjoys working, it stretches her mind and it pays the mortgage. And I don't think it was working out with us all being at home over the winter – claustrophobia was starting to set in.

• • •

We had a fun family day out today, a trip to one of our favourite haunts – the hospital. We've been back a few times for Elle's physio check-ups, but this is the first time we've been for something relating to Oliver.

During one of her visits last year, the health visitor tried to do a hearing test on the boy. She explained that the test was very sensitive and would need complete silence – not an easy task when you live close to a main road and a mainline railway. She did one ear, which was fine, then failed to get a reading for the other. She had to go to her next appointment and promised to finish next time. Then she was ill and he didn't get tested for weeks. When he did, the test failed again and so we started on the conveyor belt of NHS efficiency – we received a letter telling us to go to the hospital for a more detailed test. And we started to worry.

So there we were. The woman conducting the tests was amazed that Oliver was so old – she was expecting him to be just a few weeks. She then asked Elle to sit and rock him to sleep so that she could stick probes to his head to start the test. This was never going to happen – the more she insisted that we just needed to keep him absolutely still and silent, the more he reacted.

The woman became annoyed – she seemed to suggest that

we were deliberately trying to make the test fail and warned us that she'd have to make an official note of our lack of co-operation. Things were starting to get out of control – I immediately began to think of social services and court hearings. I got very annoyed.

Elle calmly explained the background to the test and then the penny dropped – this was a classic case of old-fashioned NHS buck passing. Something didn't happen when it should have done and we found ourselves 'bumped up' the system and wasting hospital time. The woman did the simple hearing test that had failed in our noisy house and found his hearing was perfect. We went home and within just a few hours we were able to speak without grinding our teeth.

•   •   •

March has brought an extra day's work for Elle and renewed efforts on my part to find things to do with the boy. This has become more of an issue since he started to object to his nice morning naps. It's a pain for two reasons – one, he still needs the nap, even if he doesn't know it and two, I'm no longer working on the days I'm alone with him.

Most days I make a start on something but he's awake after 20 minutes. Just to catch me out, he'll sometimes sleep for three hours, but that's only on the days when I've already given up and decided to play computer games instead. It's frustrating and I find myself getting annoyed with the situation, and tense for the rest of the day.

I've tried reversing the routine and getting him to sleep in the afternoon, but he's proving as stubborn as…well, as his father actually. The downside to creating a carbon copy of yourself is that you end up passing on the flaws too.

So in a change of tack, I'm abandoning work on my full time dad days, and I'm going to treat Oliver to an educational tour of the area. If that doesn't send the little blighter to sleep, nothing will.

• • •

Things got off to a bad start. Had I known the stone circle I was taking him to was only accessible through a couple of cow fields, I would never have attempted the journey. It also looked quite sunny when we left home, so the driving rain was an unwelcome surprise. That, the wind and the smell of cow dung combined with the crushing sense of disappointment you feel when looking at piles of broken rocks in a field. I hurt my shoulder throwing Oliver's pushchair over a hedge one handed. And I paid a pound for the privilege.

After this cultural feast, we went to see some former colleagues of mine on a local newspaper. They struggled to contain their shock at my crap social programme. But Oliver got loads of attention and cuddles from everyone. I think he enjoyed this part of the day more, though he was strangely quiet on the subject, pretending to sleep all the way home.

There was an interesting aside during our visit – one of the women asked if Oliver could have a Hobnob. "No," I replied. "He's only five months old." She nodded and thought about this, then said: "What about a Jaffa Cake, then?" This came from a woman with a couple of toddlers, and goes to show that people quickly forget about babies' development stages. That's why it's so dangerous to accept advice from anyone who claims to have been there and done it all. They usually have a dangerous combination of self-assurance and poor memory which often adds up to totally misjudged advice.

Not put off by our disastrous start, I decided to try again, this time with something a bit more meaty. So, after waiting a few days for the memory of the stones to fade, I took Oliver to his first castle.

Something odd happens to me between the planning stage and the actual trip that involves forgetting to pack all the essentials. So when we arrived at the castle, I realised I was nappyless again, and had brought nothing to drink or eat. The only accessory I'd brought was Oliver's enormous 4wd pushchair, still caked in mud from our stones tour.

On the drive, I'd been squinting in the bright spring sunshine. Getting out of the car, the first drops of rain began to hammer on the bodywork. Oliver shuddered and braced himself. If the poor lad grows up with a inbred hatred of historical monuments, he'll know who to blame. We stumbled around the few areas of the castle that the pushchair could navigate, spent some money in the shop and headed home. The cultural tour is on hold.

Carry that weight

Travelling without the pushchair

Around this time your baby is going to be wanting more variety from life than the view from the pushchair, but will also be getting pretty heavy. This was when we discovered the backpack – a tougher, more rugged version of the baby carrier that we'd been using since birth.

Oliver never really enjoyed the closeness of the small carrier, and it was hot and uncomfortable to wear, but backpacks are better for you and the baby, if a bit clumsy. When he started to rebel against the pushchair it was a useful option to have available – and it was certainly better for rough terrain and country walks.

If you're thinking about one yourself, there's a range available but I strongly recommend that you try them out in a store – some are easy to take on and off yourself with baby inside, some require the help of at least two people to put on, making them totally impractical.

• • •

I feel like I'm being pulled in two directions. In a fortnight Elle's going to be working four day weeks. She won't want to be full time carer for the other three days – and if she was we'd see nothing of each other. So my working life is fading to almost nothing. At the same time, Oliver is craving more and more attention in our time together. Slowly and surely, I feel as if I'm disappearing.

This feeling's not helped by my treatment at the hands of the people I meet while I'm out and about with Oliver. The baby clinic, where I've been taking him for fortnightly weighing sessions, is the ultimate example of a place where I simply don't exist. We arrive in the waiting area where all the mums are gathered, laughing and joking together. I sit and attempt to make small talk. Everything I say is taken as a come-on or a put-down. I give up, fall silent and wait my turn.

It's the same story in the park or at the supermarket – it's obvious that I'm either there on the pull or that I'm some kind of freak who must be avoided at all costs. I'm sure that with effort and energy I could work my way into this community, but I guess that if I have to make all the changes then it's a club I don't want to belong to. I don't feel like a full time dad, and maybe that's part of the problem. I want the best of both worlds – lots of quality time with my son and complete freedom to get on with my work. At present I'm trying to juggle both, and enjoying neither.

•   •   •

We've been on our travels again, a repeat of the ill fated UK tour we did when Oliver was six weeks old. This time we hit Manchester first, for a visit with Elle's whole family to coincide with Mothers' Day. It wasn't anything like the previous visit, when we only got a bit of sleep. This time we managed none at all, and one of the dogs got the shits all over Elle's sister's new carpet. At 5am on Mother's Day, Elle was opening her presents, Oliver was finally getting some rest and I was mopping up crap. I have a feeling there's more to life than this.

In case we hadn't learned our lesson, we headed for my parents' house for Easter. It was our last chance to get away before the start of the four day week and we refuse to give up on trips away just because they upset Oliver's routine.

It was better than before, though he still slept badly and left us both tired and grumpy. Soon the invites will start to dry up, and then we won't have to worry about going away at all. We had just enough energy left in us to toast Oliver's half-birthday. So much has happened in six months it's almost impossible to remember what life was like before, or what we were like as people.

Chapter Seven
The first year

"I feel as if my relationship with my partner is more complete after a year as parents – I have more love to give than before.", P, dad of one.

What's happening?

Six to twelve months

Your baby – While your baby will be more responsive and comfortable with you and your partner they may develop a kind of 'shyness' towards other people – even friends and relations they know fairly well. This is, in part, a realisation that the world is a bigger place than the cosy environment of home. That can be a bit intimidating at first, but it is an essential part of growing up and socialising. During this period your baby will almost certainly be eating solid food for the first time and may be developing a better sleep pattern and relying less on crying to communicate and more on other forms of contact, including touch and some very basic sounds and baby-talk.

April was a hard month. I've just about given up work, which has eased my frustration with Oliver. He's gone the other way – I can't seem to do anything to keep him happy. I try not to take it personally, but I suspect I'm just not cut out for this full time caring business.

Lack of imagination seems to be my biggest problem. I still spend my mornings trying in vain to get him to sleep – most of the time we sit and watch films. He's had a great introduction to the history of cinema – he's slept through some all time classics.

For a couple of weeks the films worked their sleep-inducing magic, then it all stopped and I had to find something else. A trip out in the car wasn't the answer as that's the trump card I always play after lunch, and a walk is my post-Countdown trick. What else is there?

Friend or foe?

The ups and downs of fatherhood

Most things that you read and hear about being a dad are focused on the tough but positive journey to understanding and appreciating each other. This suggests there's a gentle upward curve from immobile newborn to happy, responsive child. But that's not a fair picture of child development, nor is it true about relationships in general.

There will be peaks when you're completely in tune and troughs when you don't understand each other at all. And that's fine – fatherhood is a marathon, not a sprint, and you've got to expect to hit the wall eventually.

Common flashpoints come when your child is teething or during a developmental stage like learning to crawl, stand or walk. Anything that alters your child's world view has a knock-on effect on routine and relationships.

So don't be surprised if a game you play or a method you use to get the baby to sleep suddenly stops working. It's all part of the evolution process and you either need to adapt to cope or just weather the storm. But don't take it personally – the key to reaching your potential as a dad is self-confidence and that means having the good sense to see which battles you can win and which aren't worth the fight.

Life is easier with something to aim for, and at the beginning of May we're going back to the Welsh holiday cottage for another break – just the three of us. I'm going to spend the week working and swimming and generally coming back to life.

Elle needs the break just as much. She's enjoyed getting back into work mode, but since starting four day weeks she's been put under a lot of pressure to go back full time. Her company keeps messing around with her salary – they say that her part time status has confused the system. I reckon there's some resentment that she's being allowed flexible terms – the stupid thing is that if you asked the average bloke if he'd want to work less time for less money he'd probably say no. But because she appears to be getting something they aren't, they don't like it. Sheep.

The other thing she finds hard is getting home late at night and having Oliver dumped on her lap while I rush off to get some work done for an hour or so. Most of the time she's with him he's either sleepy, dopey or grumpy. Life is out of balance right now and we're all suffering the down side.

The thing I fear most of all is the effect my bad mood as

main carer is having on Oliver. I still don't feel like I'm a part of any community of parents. We're sticking with the lonely visits to the baby clinic, but I'm not getting anywhere with the mums. I chat to the neighbours and Oliver loves seeing the children run around our street, but he's five years younger than the nearest one and still just about immobile. I'd try taking him to mother and baby clubs, but I'm a bit scared of being ignored and really scared of how I will react if other children hurt or upset Oliver.

Did she fall or was she pushed?

Competitive Dad Syndrome Stage Four –

interacting with other children

My biggest fear as a self-confessed sufferer of Competitive Dad Syndrome is my son's dealings with other children.

In common with many fathers I know, I've developed an American Foreign Policy approach to interaction – I want my child to mix with the world, but I also want them to respect his special status. Unfortunately, with this approach, you just end up with a play park or toy shop filled with 'special' kids trying to dominate each other and a group of competing fathers egging them on.

The main problem with interaction is that it's too much like the cruel and cynical world of real life – and it's the first time your child shows their own personality to strangers. You want this to be a good experience, not one that involves a bop on the nose from a big kid or a telling-off from a concerned parent. But you're powerless to influence the outcome – it's like winding up a toy. All you can do is point it in the right direction, let it go, watch and hope – nature and gravity handle the rest.

Of course, there's also the issue of other children, especially how to go about stopping them from picking on your child without finding yourself picked on by a bigger daddy. Staying calm and tactful are the best bets – never try to punish a stranger's child. Simply talking to them is normally enough to make them clam up and run off to safety. Or maybe that's just me.

It's hard to tell whether Oliver's total frustration with life is a direct result of my dull efforts to amuse him, whether it's just a phase, or whether he's rejecting me out of hand. I should have watched my Hollywood blockbusters more closely – it never pays to meddle with the forces of nature. Maybe I'm not genetically programmed to care for Oliver and he's not set up to rely on me for care. If that's true, we're bound to clash – and we do.

• • •

We've had a great trip away – our first successful family holiday. Though nothing much has changed as a result of all the talking we did on holiday, we've decided that a little effort now will be rewarded later. At least we damn well hope it will.

For me to make more effort I need a bribe, and we have agreed to increase the entertainment budget a little, so Oliver and I are going to have some slightly more adventurous trips out. We've got zoo membership, National Trust membership and a year long pass to the safari park. We're going to sightsee until we drop.

This parade of heritage and amusement isn't going to ease Elle's headache at work, but it'll mean she's less likely to come home to a desperate husband and a bored child.

• • •

Things have become a bit easier. I'm still likely to forget essential items for our trips out, we're still followed around the countryside by a giant rain cloud. Oliver is still faintly confused by the places I take him. But life is at least varied.

It would be even better if we had some people to talk to. We wander up and down the patch of grass along our road hoping to catch the eye of some poor sod for me to engage in conversation for an hour or so. The front gardens of all our neighbours' houses have become overgrown wastelands as people shelter round the back to avoid me. Curtains twitch nervously as we approach. I've managed to combine being both bored and boring.

As with so much of my life, this period of childcare would have been wonderful and successful had I thought about it first. But as it is, I'm stuck with what I've got and forced to make the best of it.

On the horizon is a real glimmer of hope and bonding session rolled into one. Father's Day is nearly here – and hard on its heels is our first summer football tournament.

•   •   •

In an act of clear friendship, Oliver bought me a novelty football for Father's Day. It was a good day – though it still seems totally unreal to think of myself as a father. Talking to my dad about Oliver is such a weird concept, and yet I can't get enough of the excitement I feel when talking about 'my son', or 'my boy'. It makes me sound so grown up.

Which, obviously, is why I took him straight to the sports shop to get matching England kits. On the day of the first game of the tournament, we paraded around the living room in our Red and Whites, kicking the novelty football with great enthusiasm. And then Oliver went to bed, I watched the game, we lost and I swore bitterly.

He was awake for the next game, but was very tired. He screamed with terror every time we celebrated a goal or shouted at the ref. His face was a picture of misery and was as red as his shirt. Suddenly, I felt terribly guilty for forcing him to play along with something he neither enjoyed nor understood.

Sitting with my son on my knee cheering our team to glory is one of the great clichés of becoming a dad which I'd pictured before he was born – it's all about me and nothing to do with him, or with reality. It'll never happen, at least not in the way I imagine it, because life isn't about predictable, planned experiences. If I want him to grow up blue, he'll grow up red and vice versa – and if I try to decide his behaviour I'll fail dismally. A bit like the football team, then.

• • •

Life has suddenly turned on its head. Elle has become very frustrated with her work. I think they were expecting the pre-baby Elle to reappear magically and start taking charge all over again. But that's not happened and it's frustrated her, frustrated them and has made working part time almost impossible. With no alternative, she's decided to leave her job.

Before she became pregnant we built up some savings to cope in the event of her not going back after maternity leave. It's a great relief to have that buffer, especially as I'm now the main wage earner. Last time I sent in a tax return, the Inland Revenue sent back a food parcel. I don't make enough money to cover the cost of the electricity I'm using to write this sentence.

My wage was never meant to be the sole source of our income, but now it has to be. To keep us afloat I need to be dynamic, focused and driven. Time to sell the house.

Actually, there is another prospect on the horizon –

though not a really profitable one. I've managed to get work at a university summer school where I taught last year. It's only part time at first, and lasts just a couple of months, but it meets the main objective of putting off any real decisions over what to do next.

• • •

Things are going OK. I got through the part time hours no problem – Elle and the boy love being together again and they've been off for long walks in the mornings while I've been at the college. In the afternoons we've been going out as a family. Yet again we found ourselves in the blissful, unreal environment we enjoyed for those first few months.

Then the full time days started and the roles shifted once more. During last year's tutoring, I was careful not to mention Elle or the pregnancy. Many of my students were Japanese, and they can be very earnest about their study. Anything that suggests the tutor is not one hundred per cent focused can lead to problems. So I was the total professional.

This year, I tried. I waited until well after morning break

on day one before getting out my photos of Oliver. I am totally, boringly proud of him and I'm always happy to stop lessons to talk about his every waking moment. I'm away from him for a matter of hours each day and yet I miss him terribly. This is really costly on the days out that form part of the course, which I use as an excuse to load up with souvenirs for my little boy – so much for the main wage earner.

After moaning endlessly for three months about looking after Oliver, I've suddenly become an expert in childcare. I offer advice to Elle at every opportunity. She replies with different, slightly more direct and certainly more painful offers.

Despite my crappy advice, she's been having few problems looking after Oliver during these full days, though he has reached the age where he wants to do everything, but is capable of almost nothing. He crawls and babbles, but longs to walk and speak. He has endless energy and a complete inability to take naps on demand.

He's also going through a teething marathon which started in May and has rolled on for a couple of months. On the downside he's often grumpy and his carefully structured sleep routine has slipped a bit, but on the plus side teething has given us a 'one size fits all' excuse for bad behaviour. Tantrum in the street? He's teething. Destroying his granny's latest gift? He's teething. Launching a pre-emptive nuclear strike on Moscow? He's teething. By the time we've finished using this excuse Oliver will be a teenager and will have something in the region of five thousand teeth.

•   •   •

Last weekend marked the mid-point of my full time teaching and Saturday was a lovely summer's day. Elle and I took Oliver down the road to one of the local pubs, where we sat in the sun and shared a bottle of wine. Oliver drank his juice. All was right with the world. Elle was relaxed and calm, I was making some money. Oliver was well and happy. Why the hell didn't I suspect something?

Saturday night he went to bed with no problems. In the middle of the night he woke and was violently sick all over his cot. We took him downstairs and he was sick again a couple more times. It was horrible to watch, but eventually he calmed down enough to settle back to sleep. We lay awake and listened to him for hours.

Sunday he seemed a little better. He didn't eat or drink much, but he wasn't throwing up. Whatever was upsetting him seemed to have passed. On Monday he was worse. He was sick again and this time Elle decided to take him to the doctor. I was at work, but my mind was at home. The doctor said it was a bug and that he'd be OK. Relief all round.

By Tuesday he'd got much worse. He barely woke all day and when I got home from work, he sat on my lap, ate a rusk and promptly threw it back up all over my trousers. We headed for the doctor again and this time he wasn't so sure all was well. He told us to go straight to the hospital, and gave us a note to pass to the people in the children's ward. Oliver clung to us, pale, limp and spaced out. I felt sick too, and very, very empty.

Emergency ward Zen

Staying calm in hospital

No father wants to imagine the trauma and pain involved in a medical emergency for their child. But it's a fair bet that sometime in the next few months and years something will happen that leaves you facing your fears in a hospital.

Whether it's an overnight stay, or a quick (quick? ha!) trip to casualty, your role in this situation is closely linked to the job you did during your partner's labour. You need to be the rock, the source of comfort and stability, regardless of your internal fears.

If your partner is focused on your baby's well-being, you'll have to keep a line of communication going with medical staff – and that means keeping yourself calm. Even in the slightly more relaxed surroundings of a ward, the staff are under extreme pressure and they shouldn't be sidetracked or dominated without good reason.

At the same time, you've got to look after your child's needs – and you aren't there to make lifelong friends. If you have to complain or gee people up, try to be firm and calm and never aggressive.

If your partner is anything like Elle, you'll also have to remind her to eat, drink and sleep. She'll need a break from her care, but might be reluctant to take one – be firm and tactful.

Beyond this supporting role there's little you can practically do once you're in the hospital. That can leave you feeling a bit redundant, or even guilty but, thinking back to the delivery suite again, your active presence is all that's required.

At the hospital I almost broke my strict 'no murdering the nurses' rule. We stumbled onto the ward through the wrong entrance, Oliver was on his hands and knees, throwing up all over the floor when a nurse approached, firstly to tell us that we'd come through the wrong door and then to say that she thought Oliver looked unwell.

"Yes," I said, just about choking back the words 'no shit, Florence'. "Can you help us, then?" I added.

"Well I'm not actually on duty yet," she replied. She did, honestly. And I got up from where my son was coughing and spluttering on the floor and I wrenched her head clean off and kicked it down the corridor. Something in my eyes must have hinted at that outcome, because she was suddenly on duty and ready to take us seriously.

Oliver was almost lifeless. We laid him on the bed and he barely moved. His skin was grey, his eyes were sunken and he was unresponsive. Even the newly available nurse was worried. After much prodding and poking by doctors it was decided he should be put on a drip. He was taken away to have a needle inserted in his arm. Elle went with him. I wouldn't have been able to stand it. Pathetic, I know, but this was not the time for false heroism.

I could hear his screams from across the ward. I didn't know he had it left in him. When they came back about 15 minutes later, his arms and legs were bandaged from all the wounds they'd made trying to find a decent vein.

The nurse brought in the drip and its monitor. This kept stalling and having to be reset. With a skeleton staff working overnight, we were waiting five minutes or more every time for the staff to come and deal with the machine, which gave off a piercing whine when it wasn't happy. And each delay meant it would take longer to hydrate him. My fraying nerves couldn't stand it. The doctor came back and checked on Oliver. He said it was simply a case of waiting to see what effect the drip would have. He offered us no comfort, but he didn't seem unduly worried either. He asked us what Oliver's last meal had been. When we said it was a rusk, he replied: "Oh lovely, I'm 32, but I still like rusks."

My jaw dropped. Thirty-two? That's my age, and I haven't a clue what to do to bring my son back to health. I'm desperate and anxious in equal measures and the responsibility for care of our child has been passed to a teenager, a trainee. I wanted to demand a doctor with at least 50 years' experience. I waited until he'd gone and I told Elle that we should complain. She told me I should go home. I went home.

This morning there wasn't much change. Elle barely slept last night, and nor did I. The world has a surreal, dream-like hue. I've been feeling ill, but Elle's well of sympathy has been drained by the beeping of the faulty drip monitor and another long, painful attempt to get Oliver's drip needle repositioned.

After sitting in silence for a couple of hours, I went home again. I was feeling much worse. I emptied my stomach's contents through every available orifice and sat in the bathroom shivering. I stared at my reflection in the mirror – my lips were blue. I took some tablets and laid on the sofa.

When I woke a couple of hours later I felt much better, so I went back to the hospital. Oliver was sitting on Elle's lap when I arrived; he looked up at me and smiled and my heart burst into a thousand grateful pieces.

By way of a parting shot, the doctor told us that Oliver has been suffering from some kind of bacterial bug, possibly even meningitis, but that he'll be fine with a few days' rest. My immediate instinct was to complain that we should have been told this before now. But then I remembered my erratic behaviour of last night and I was grateful to them for keeping a lid on my panic for another 24 hours.

Until these last few days, I wouldn't have believed there was anything that parenthood could throw at us which we couldn't handle. I thought we knew it all – that we'd built the confidence, the experience and the knowledge to deal with every situation. How could I have been so wrong?

Oliver's illness might have knocked my confidence, but it's also going to stop me taking him for granted. When my summer school ends I'll be a better father, more fun, more responsible, less fretful and stressed. I'll double the number of pictures in my wallet and triple the extent to which I bore strangers. I'll do whatever it takes, just as long as he stays safe and healthy.

•   •   •

The scare over Oliver's health has been a setback. It's a reminder of those first few weeks when we worried over every little thing, every speck of dust or dirt. Though he's crawling and clambering all over the house, we follow close behind, fearful that he will pick up some awful bug.

It's hardly fair to use my son's illness as an excuse for my laziness, but over the last month I've spent a lot of time with him. It's partly due to the guilt I feel at letting him get ill, and partly to Elle needing a well earned break from full time childcare.

Despite the occasional difficulty – 'he's teething' – Elle and Oliver have really bonded during these summer months together. Maybe my desire to be with him now is also a wish to stay up to speed with his development. I'm delighted things have changed, that Elle is at home, but I'm sad that my time with Oliver wasn't more of a success. I miss the closeness that we shared, even when things weren't going well.

He's got a couple of major milestones coming up, both on the same day. We're throwing him a lunchtime party for his first birthday and then, in the evening, we're taking him on the ferry to Ireland for his first trip overseas. It might be wonderful, it might be a disaster.

Spread your wings

Travelling abroad with the baby

Overseas travel with a baby can be a great experience, but only if you've made good provision. Here's the essentials:

Snap decision. First of all you're going to need a passport for the baby. There's no getting around this anymore, which means you'll have to somehow manage the Herculean task of getting your kid to sit still and look smart for five seconds while you capture a passport photo. Trying to do this in a photo booth is downright impossible – so do it at home. Follow the guidelines from the passport application leaflet available at the Post Office.

The secret's in the timing. A long-haul journey is a complete nightmare with a wide-awake, bored and angry baby, so try to dovetail the bulk of the travel with a scheduled nap. Most babies are pretty skilled at sleeping just about anywhere, so you might as well take advantage of some downtime.

Choose wisely. It stands to reason that you'll have a better chance of a successful holiday in a family-friendly location, but that doesn't necessarily relegate you to theme parks for all eternity. There's a massive range of hotels and B&Bs at home and abroad (and particularly in the

US, where almost everything is child-friendly) that provide excellent facilities for babies, from the expected cot in the room to the more surprising baby listening facilities, bottle warming services and even soft play areas.

Shopping trips. You may struggle to find exact matches for baby food, formula milk and nappies in foreign shops, so if you're attached to a particular brand, take it with you. If you're going on a long haul flight or boat trip, try to get confirmation that a cot will be provided – you don't want to be carrying the baby for 10 hours. Some travel companies will book a cot for you, others prefer to watch parents fight it out in a first come, first served gladiatorial contest. If you don't fancy that, take your own travel cot.

Get covered. You'll always need travel insurance – and make sure everyone's covered – but if you're just travelling in the EU, you can also apply for a European Health Insurance Card which gives a big discount in healthcare charges in member states. Details can be obtained from Post Offices and travel agents. Remember that you need to apply for each family member. Further information on travel – including vaccination of children and babies, can be found on the Foreign and Commonwealth office website (www.fco.gov.uk).

•   •   •

Or it might be both. Unlike his quiet first day in the world, his first birthday has been a spectator sport. Both sets of grandparents had ringside seats, giving the event a competitive edge.

The grandfathers were dignified and cool, with just the odd rustle of newspaper telling us they were still awake. But the grannies rolled up their sleeves and went head-to-head in an old-fashioned bout of 'Oliver Monopoly'. It's a cruel, sometimes vicious sport, and I'm surprised Sky hasn't snapped up the TV rights. But in truth it was good natured stuff and Oliver had a wonderful time basking in all the attention.

Then it was present time, and the grannies retreated to their corners. I sat on the floor with Oliver as the grandparents took it in turns to produce larger and larger presents, each trumping the last, until he and I were lost in a sea of wrapping and plastic activity sets.

Finally it was time for lunch – a great spread cooked up by Elle. All this attention grabbing had given Oliver an appetite and he ploughed into his sandwiches and cake. After five minutes of happy munching we were all congratulating ourselves on a decent party. And to cap it all

Oliver fell asleep mid-bite. We settled him in his pushchair, cake still in hand, and he woke an hour later and resumed eating as if he'd just been switched back on.

There was a temptation, and a bit of pressure, to invite neighbouring children to the party, or to cast around for all the people we know with kids of similar ages. But Oliver's too young for all that nonsense – we face years of strange smelling ugly kids trampling cake through our house and expecting a goody bag in return. I'm not going to hasten that nightmare, just because it's expected of us as loving parents.

It's my party and I'll cry...

Keeping a lid on birthdays

In all honesty the first birthday party should be filed under Competitive Dad Syndrome – if it wasn't for the fact that mums are just as guilty of over egging this particular celebratory pudding.

There's nothing wrong with throwing a huge party for your one year old, but don't pretend it's actually for the child themselves. Your baby will probably sleep through half of it, dividing the remainder of the time between indifference and terror. At 12 months a baby can certainly

enjoy the company of other children, but it's yet to be scientifically ver-
ified that they enjoy passing the parcel.

The first birthday party is all about showing off – you're happy that your
parenting skills have got your child to this landmark, and you want to
broadcast that fact to the world. Fine, but don't plan a huge extrava-
ganza if you aren't prepared for your child to get bored within five minutes, or throw up at an unfortunate moment.

Don't let it become a matter of great stress, involving outside catering
and portable loos. No-one will think any worse of you as a father and
your child won't remember a thing in any case. It's good sense to ask
someone to record the highlights of the party on video – especially if
you're missing key events while running around topping up drinks and
serving food. Don't be tempted to shoot the video yourself, or you'll
miss even more of the party.

Anyway, how many kids get a holiday to Ireland as a birthday present? Not many, I'll wager – because not many parents are foolish enough to take their cake stuffed children
on rough sea voyages way past their bedtime.

But that's exactly what we're doing. Oliver had a bit of a
tantrum in the car, and he's been almost impossible to set-

tle in our 'deluxe' cabin right over the bow doors. One of the ship's PA speakers is just outside the cabin door, booming out rolling adverts for the cinema and Paddy O'Themepub's good time bar.

Elle is resigned to another long night and has agreed to sleep with Oliver in her bunk. I can't sleep at all, so I wandered the corridors of the ship, stopped at Paddy's for a quick pint, then returned to the cabin to read in my bunk.

It's 11.04pm I've been looking at my watch for the last five minutes, waiting for the hands to inch round. Exactly one year ago this minute, my son was introduced to the world. I've been trying to remember exactly how I felt back then. The boat is rocking, and the beer has made me dizzy. My stomach lurches and I'm severely short of sleep. Yep, that was it. Fatherhood in a nutshell – everything is different and nothing changes. What a ride.

Chapter Eight
One year and counting

"Always be hands-on with everything. You've got to believe that you're just as good at everything as your partner." G, dad of three.

What's happening?

Twelve to eighteen months

Your baby – The fact that the word 'toddler' is beginning to be thrown about with regard to your baby should give you a clue as to the next key developmental stage. Toddling, or walking with added bounce, is a skill most babies acquire somewhere between their first and second birthdays. It doesn't really matter when they get there, what's important is that this is a strike for freedom and independence. Your baby will be forming more words, including some recognisable ones, and will be absorbing new information on a daily basis. They will begin to remember details and will understand (though won't necessarily respond to) simple instructions. Some fairly ambitious souls feel that the 12-18 month period is the right time to introduce potty training as well, though this should really only be done if your baby shows a willingness to participate. Your baby should be sleeping fairly well by now, with maybe just one daytime nap to back up a good night's sleep. Food should be pretty wide ranging, with your baby now able to eat just about everything you can – though it might be worth steering clear of the vindaloo.

The records show that Oliver took his first tentative steps on a beautiful, empty beach in County Kerry. He took to the idea almost immediately and by the time we were back from Ireland he was starting to make a break for independence.

I don't know whether the strange rollercoaster of Oliver's first year has had any negative impact on his development. The changes in main carer might have been a bad thing, but it's helped him get used to both our styles of parenting, and it means we're a more effective unit. He calls us both 'mum'. I'm proud of that, pleased to say that I can spend quality time with my son without it being a terrific stress. I still try to take him to bookshops and on cultural trips. He still hates them.

While we continue to find ways to improve the work/life balance, we do feel we've got the balance of care just about right. We always aimed at 50-50 childcare and right now it's about 60-40, with Elle taking the larger share. When she's back working again, the balance will shift once more, but neither of us plans to be a full time carer again.

In other ways our family life has taken on an oddly traditional edge. Oliver comes to me for play, to his mother for hugs and comfort. No matter what I do, no matter what any father does, mum will always be number one and part of the reason for my relaxed attitude is the fact that I've finally come to accept that and try to work on my relationship with Oliver instead.

Now he's mobile, he loves to race around the neighbourhood and I can't resist the temptation to show him off all over again. He has an entire cupboard filled with footballs I've bought him to practice with.

I'm passing more than just my sporting hopes onto the

boy. He's become such a sponge for information, soaking up new words and noises. I have to be very careful about the phrases I choose around him – especially those which I apply to certain members of the family. I know that one day this charming game of parrots will bite me on the arse when he happily repeats some choice expression.

Until then, I'm just enjoying the experience of having a playmate that I can be totally stupid with. We come up with ridiculous games, we try to trump each other with the volume of our 'raspberry' fart noises and we mess around at the table.

The last of these games has been a cause of some concern in the house. As Oliver moves from a milk based diet to more solids, he needs to start learning some table manners – not easy with me gurning at him all the time. Elle has to play the grown-up to get us both to eat properly. I know it's not fair, I know it undermines a vital element of her parenting, but it also demonstrates a vital part of mine – it's great to have someone around who thinks you're a genius for making fart sounds.

Joined-up parenting is tough to put into action, but I do appreciate how unfair it is that I'm always undermining

Elle's attempts to impose rules and limits on Oliver's behaviour. It's also very confusing for the boy.

Dads are the usual culprits when it comes to this kind of misbehaviour because we generally have limited time with our children and want it to be as enjoyable as possible. Don't want your dinner? Have a biscuit instead. Result, I'm a hero for a few minutes and Elle's carefully designed nutrition plan goes out the window. It's neither fair nor constructive and it won't actually help me in the long run – I'll just end up with a son who's an expert in playing me off against his mother.

Do you know who I am?

Discipline and the toddler

Being balanced and fair. Despite the apparently angelic exterior, toddlers are actually pretty damn good at being naughty, and the concept of discipline, which you probably assumed would never arise in your prodigy's development, is now likely to be a hot subject. One of the main problems you face with discipline is the one outlined above – the good cop, bad cop approach which puts mum in the role of the harsh disciplinarian and dad in the role of everyone's best mate. Though this pattern of behaviour won't scar your child for life, there's a chance that your partner's fists may scar you at least in the short term. In short, it isn't fair on her and doesn't lead to any improvement in your child's behaviour.

While the co-operative approach is the best way forward, that doesn't mean there's any real harm in establishing authority figures in your child's life. Speaking personally, as a child I was always more frightened by the threat that my father would be told about my behaviour 'when he gets home' than by any real punishment given out when he did. If your partner works, swap 'dad' for 'mum' as the final arbiter of justice, but the effect should be the same. Yes, it would be better if everyone sat around in a circle and discussed their feelings calmly but toddlers are simple souls and they need boundaries.

Setting realistic punishments. As a parent you can't help tuning in to other people's attempts to discipline their children. Sometimes I pick up a really good point, sometimes I cringe with ill-concealed horror. One thing that always gets my back up is the wild over-reaction punishment along the lines of: 'stop picking your nose right now or we'll cut short our Greek holiday right now and I'll charter a private plane home.' If that isn't an invitation to have a good old rake around up your nostril I don't know what is. If you're going to threaten a punishment, make it tangible and simple – and be sure you will be able to follow it through. There's no point in making a threat that both you and the child know will never be acted upon, that jut undermines your authority and makes you seem daft. And seeming daft in the eyes of an eighteen-month-old child is not good.

Coping with tantrums. When the first tantrum hits it is a bit of a shock, in the same way that an earthquake registering 9.0 on the Richter Scale is a bit of a shock. Who knew that this quiet, unassuming baby could produce such an unappealing combination of screams, crimson face, tears, snot and associated bodily fluids simply because no-one will allow them to ride on next door's doggy? The fact that this emotional El Nino can strike anywhere – in the street, at a wedding, in the shops, during the final of the snooker world championships – makes it even more frightening. So how do you handle a public display? A recent TV advert showed a parent throwing a huge tantrum in a supermarket and her embarrassed child slinking away, and you could always take this pre-emptive approach if you've got the guts. Personally, I think might be going a bit far.

But the theory is good in the sense that you need to distract your child from whatever is causing the tantrum. It may be that you have the perfect opportunity if there's something notable to point out ('look, there goes a fire engine') or it may be that you have to grin, bear it and keep plugging away with a relentlessly happy exterior while childless oafs gather round to tut at you. Don't rise to the bait and shout at your child, it will only make things worse.

If you're at home things may be a bit easier as you have the opportunity to ignore the tantrum by just leaving it to burn itself out. The older a child gets, the more violent tantrums can become and the most maddening kind are those when your child goes into 'rag-doll' mode and won't stand up straight. Again, you have very little option but to let it pass as long as your child won't come to any harm rolling about on the floor.

In the six months since his first birthday, he's gone from being a baby to a proper, fully fledged boy. He's become an individual who still has his fair share of tantrums, bumps and bruises, but who is also putting words and thoughts together, making connections and understanding the world around him. It's fascinating to watch the way his mind is developing and how he is beginning to find more sophisticated ways to communicate – although at the moment these do consist of a series of incredibly accurate animal sounds.

With me as a father it's incredible that he's as amazing as he is today. But I can only appreciate just how amazing he is because I made sure I was there for the whole journey – I was even in the driving seat for some of it.

My first year as a dad wasn't about dominating the nappy changes, or proving I could be Elle's equal as a mother – it wasn't even just about having fun – it was about settling comfortably into a relationship with my son, and realising how far it could take me.

Looking back over this first year, I'm surprised at how I've turned out as a dad – at different times I've been more anxious, more hands-on, more serious and responsible. It's been a voyage of self-discovery – but not one that's set in stone. I continue to think about what I expected from fatherhood and whether I've met those expectations. In some ways I have, in other areas I really want to change – I'm very keen to give him more space and allow his personality to flourish.

I haven't enjoyed every part of this tough first year – particularly the medical emergencies and the stress of Oliver's various 'growth spurts' but that doesn't put me off – there'll still be ups and downs but I know it's going to get easier and the rewards are going to be greater. I even find it a little easier to talk to other dads without bullshitting now, especially since I learned to embrace and manage my competitive edge – 'my name is Stephen and I have Competitive Dad Syndrome'.

In fact I have started to re-establish a few old social connections. My mates and I take part in a pub quiz and though I invariably begin the evening with an anecdote about how well Oliver went to bed, or how he has picked up the endearing habit of sticking his fingers up his nose, they do just smile and nod, safe in the knowledge that the Guinness will start to kick in after the second pint and I will start thinking less about babies and more about 'who sang Britain's 1990 Eurovision song contest entry?'

The whole process of becoming a dad was a culture shock in itself, but it's settling down a bit now and we're becoming good friends. I particularly love bedtime, telling Oliver little stories or singing songs in his darkened bedroom. The only downside to this is that there's a rather comfy bed to lie on in his room, so I often find myself waking up after half an hour's doze with the poor little fellow sound asleep. Naturally, I then go downstairs and complain about how long it took to settle him.

• • •

Now that life is calming down another question has been doing the rounds at our place. Does Oliver need a sibling? Given our fondness for living in wild and uninhabited parts of the country the answer ought to be a clear yes – despite my repeated assurances that I'm the only company he will ever need, he did ought to have playmates more his own age.

But there's a lot to consider – not least the impact on our relationship, on the relationship we're building with Oliver, and the fact that we'd need to buy one of those crappy people movers if we ever want to go anywhere. Generally speaking, friends and relations seem to think we've been incredibly lucky with Oliver. He is certainly a good boy, maybe another baby would be a nightmare – showing the whole world that Oliver's excellent behaviour is just a fluke and we are, in fact, terrible parents.

Four's company

Having a second child

It's been said that a second child fills up all the gaps in your time that a first child leaves, and as you're probably feeling like your life is pretty full of child-related activities right now you might be forgiven for thinking about stopping at one.

Naturally, there's pros and cons of larger families and most of them are related to your individual circumstances. But there's a couple of general points to consider before you start the ball rolling once more:

Are you up to it? I'm not just talking about the physical endeavour of another pregnancy and the impact this will have on you and, more directly, your partner. I'm talking about the fact that when baby number two is born you will have to devote a lot more of your time to your first child, and that will have an impact on your free time and on your energy levels. If you thought that you needed to be fit to have a baby, try lugging two of them through a supermarket while pushing a trolley with your hips.

The cost implication. You may find that a second child makes very little difference to your household costs, especially if you've already budgeted for one of you to be home full time. Most of the baby equipment you used first time round will still be OK to use, but a second child may well necessitate a change in car, house and possibly childcare arrangements – while a tame granny might be happy looking after one little one, two becomes a much bigger and more demanding role.

Bonding issues. You've worked hard to build a firm bond with your first child and it will be hard, though not impossible, for them not to feel the impact of their sibling's arrival. You need to think very carefully about how you manage the amount of information and involvement you want your first child to have during the pregnancy. It's a huge generalisation of course, but little girls seem to adapt to the idea of a baby much more easily. Little boys find sharing the attentions of their mother harder and so as a result they can become quite competitive and their behaviour can suffer. Be understanding and try to ensure that both you and your partner get to spend lots of quality time with your first child both during the pregnancy and afterwards. You have a special bond with your first born which will never break, but at the same time, you need to reassure them that all will be well.

Most of all, I wonder whether I'd be prepared for another nine months of living like a spare part, dealing with all the emergencies, fears, costs and medical personnel and then going through the sleepless nights and powerless fears of early fatherhood once again.

Looking at it this way, the answer's simple – having another baby would count as certifiable madness. But then again…

Contact us

You're welcome to contact White Ladder Press if you have any questions or comments for either us or the authors. Please use whichever of the following routes suits you.

Phone: **0208 334 1600**

Email: **enquiries@whiteladderpress.com**

Fax: **0208 334 1601**

Address: **2nd Floor, Westminster House, Kew Road, Richmond, Surrey TW9 2ND**

Website: **www.whiteladderpress.com**

What can our website do for you?

If you want more information about any of our books, you'll find it at **www.whiteladderpress.com**. In particular you'll find extracts from each of our books, and reviews of those that are already published. We also run special offers on future titles if you order online before publication. And you can request a copy of our free catalogue.

Many of our books have links pages, useful addresses and so on relevant to the subject of the book. You'll also find out a bit more about us and, if you're a writer yourself, you'll find our submission guidelines for authors. So please check us out and let us know if you have any comments, questions or suggestions.

From **Lad** to **Dad**

New Edition

The ultimate guide to pregnancy for blokes

Stephen Giles

OK, your partner's pregnant. Congratulations, that's great news. You're The Man, back of the net! You'll make a great dad, and life will be great. Different, but still great. Won't it?

From Lad to Dad is a guide for men whose partners are pregnant. Pregnancy changes women. Big time. Not all the changes are obvious. Or good. This book guides you through what's normal and what's not. How you use that knowledge is up to you, but telling your partner that most couples have sex three times a day when they're newly pregnant probably won't wash.

Let's face it, there's some important stuff you need to know:

- **baby:** Is it safe and well? And more importantly, can you get it to support your team by playing Sky Sports to it while it's growing inside your Mrs?
- **breasts:** How big will they get? How long will they stay that size? And are they strictly off-limits?
- **car:** How sensible, exactly, does it have to be?
- **sex:** How much is OK, now and, err, later on. And will it still be the same?
- **cash:** OK, it's going to hurt, but how badly?
- **d-day:** It's happening. Yikes! Can I stay up the head end? Will she be OK afterwards? And still, well, interested…?
- **hormones:** Remember, whatever the question, the answer's 'Yes'… or 'No', or whatever she wants it to be.
- **life after baby:** Will you ever be able to sleep again? Without getting drunk? Will you ever be able to get drunk again?

Written by a normal bloke after consultation with his mates and their mates and many more blokes who've survived it.

£8.99

Cool, Calm Parent

How not to lose it with your kids

There's no shortage of advice out there on how to deal with your children's tantrums, but what about your own?

Many parents are reluctant to admit it, but an awful lot of us have trouble controlling our own temper when the kids are unruly. Maybe not all the time, but more often than we'd choose. Obviously we don't *like* yelling at the kids, it's just that we can't help ourselves.

At last, Hollie Smith has written a book that fesses up to the problem, and looks at practical techniques to help us keep a lid on the anger and set our kids the example we want to. She enlists the help of psycholgists and anger management experts to find plenty of strategies that help to avoid trouble in the first place. However, recognising that most of us lose it with our kids from time to time, she also helps us find ways to:

- mind our language
- resist the urge to get physical
- button up before we say anything we'll regret
- patch it up afterwards
- find a cooler, calmer lifestyle

Cool, Calm Parent is also packed with case studies and quotes from real, everyday parents like you and me. The kind who want to be cool and calm with our kids, but don't quite manage it all the time.

£9.99